Tranquil scene looking west towards the Tramroad Bridge – 1860s.
(*Harris Ref. Lib.*)

# The Old Tram Road

*Walton Summit to Preston Basin*

STEPHEN BARRITT

Carnegie Publishing Ltd

© S. Barritt, 2000

First published in 2000 by
Carnegie Publishing
Carnegie House
Chatsworth Road
Lancaster
LA1 4SL

All rights reserved
Unauthorised duplication
contravenes existing laws

ISBN 1–85936–058–0

Typeset in Minion and Caslon Antique by
Carnegie Publishing, Lancaster
Printed and bound by
T. Snape and Co. Ltd, Preston

# Foreword

Today, the best known monument to the Lancaster Canal Tramroad is the distinctive precast concrete trestle bridge spanning the River Ribble and connecting Avenham Park with the handsome tree lined walkway which heads southwards across the expansive Ribble valley flood plane.

For many years I associated the tramroad with the electric tramcar, which proliferated around the turn of the century, and had assumed that the Old Tram Road originally formed part of an electric powered mass transit system ferrying people in and out of Preston.

This notion was far from the truth. The tramroad had ceased operating long before the electric tram appeared on our streets, and pre-dates the railways by some thirty five years.

After realising the antiquity of the tramroad and its importance in the development of the North West of England I resolved to delve further into its history.

This book is the culmination of ten years (on and off) research, and charts the fortunes of the tramroad from its inception at the close of the eighteenth century through to modern times.

Much of the detail is gleaned from source documents and drawings retained in the Lancashire Record Office and the Public Record Office at Kew in London.

## *Acknowledgements*

I am indebted to Gordon Biddle whose early work inspired me to start this book and who helped me enormously towards its conclusion by offering much needed constructive criticism and by allowing me to publish some of his own photographs.

Thanks also to David Hunt, eminent local author and curator of the South Ribble Museum and Exhibition Centre (well worth a visit) for allowing me access to the exhibits and for pointing me in the right direction on a number of occasions, and to Barry Dutton of Autosave for his photographs and background details relating to the tramroad at Bamber Bridge.

I would like to mention the staff of Lancashire Record Office, Public Record Office, Lancashire County Books, Harris Museum and Art Gallery, Harris Reference Library, Lancaster Reference Library, Institution of Civil Engineers and the Railway and Canal Historical Society who I always found very welcoming and helpful. In particular Louise Connel and Vincent Kelly at the Harris, Susan Halstead at Library Headquarters, Ann Dennison at the Harris Library and Carol Morgan at the I.C.E..

The illustrations occupy a significant proportion of this book and I am indebted to the following; Lancaster Reference Library, Harris Museum and Art Gallery, Lancashire County Library: Harris Library, Lancashire Record Office, South Ribble Museum and Exhibition Centre, Public Record Office, Gordon Biddle, John Garlington's *Preston a Photographic Record*, Anthony Hewitson's *History of Preston 1883*, Ordnance Survey, Andrew Iley and Barry Dutton.

When I was looking for a publisher I went to Carnegie first. During my research I read a variety of local history books and it became clear that those published by Carnegie were the most attractive and well produced. That standard has been carried through into this book and I would like to thank all the staff for transforming my efforts into this smart publication.

# Introduction

In 1792 an Act of Parliament was passed for the construction of the Lancaster Canal. The canal would link, and pass through the towns of Wigan, Preston, Lancaster and Kendal. Its main purpose was to enable the supply of cheap coal to the north and cheap limestone to the south.

The cutting of canals over level ground was comparatively inexpensive, but where hills and valleys were encountered, the costs would rocket. The Ribble valley presented a formidable obstacle which was to be overcome by the construction of 32 locks in order to lower the canal 222ft from Walton Summit to the level at Preston. In addition, a massive stone aqueduct was to be constructed to carry the canal across the river.

The canal company understandably opted for cutting the level lengths of canal first, and the contractors were set to work to the north and south of Preston.

By 1799 the 'easy' parts of the canal were complete and the problem of crossing the Ribble valley came to the fore. At this juncture the company found itself in an impossible situation: there was now insufficient funding to traverse the valley, and the truncated canal was not in a position to earn sufficient income to make a profit.

A cheaper alternative was sought to cross the valley, and after much deliberation the committee reluctantly agreed to the construction of a tramroad in order to temporarily connect the two ends of the canal, with the intention of replacing it with the originally envisaged waterway when sufficient income had been generated in tolls.

The tramroad took three years to construct and was open for business towards the end of 1803. It comprised of a dual cast iron plateway upon which horses pulled trains of up to six waggons, each carrying two tons of coal or limestone.

The slopes at Avenham, Carr Wood and Walton Summit were thought too steep for the horses to negotiate, and here stationary steam winding engines were installed in order to haul the waggons by means of an endless chain.

Despite every effort, the canal company never did find sufficient capital to finance the construction of a canal across the Ribble valley, and the tramroad ran successfully for over seventy five years before it was swallowed up by the all pervading steam locomotive operated railway.

The new millenium has brought a new twist to the story. Ironically, a scheme similar to one originally suggested in 1800 as an alternative to the tramroad is being progressed to enable barges to pass between the Lancaster Canal and the Leeds & Liverpool via the River Douglas, the Ribble estuary and a new length of canal linking the Ribble to the Lancaster Canal.

# Weights and Measures

This publication includes many references to the old monetary system and also to imperial weights and measures. For the benefit of readers under the age of 40, I have listed the old imperial system with their metric equivalents in italics.

## Money

£1 = 20s (shillings)
1s = 12d (old pence)
*1s = 5p (new pence)*
*1d = 0.417p (new pence)*

## Length/Distance

1 mile = 1760yds (yards)
1 furlong = 220yds
1 chain = 220yds
1 rood = 16.5ft (feet)
1yd = 3ft
1ft = 12in. (inches)
*1 mile = 1.609Km*
*1yd = 91.4cm*
*1ft = 30.46cm*
*1in. = 2.54cm*

## Area

1 square mile = 640 acres
1 acre = 4840 sq. yds (square yards)
1 rood = 1210 sq. yds
1 square perch = 30.25 sq. yds
1 sq. yd = 9 sq. ft (square feet)
1 sq. ft = 144 sq. ins (square inches)
*1 acre = 0.405 ha.*
*1 sq. yd = 0.836 sq. m.*
*1 sq. in. = 6.452 sq. cm*

## Volume

1 cub. yd (cubic yard) = 27 cub. ft (cubic feet)
1 cub. ft = 1728 cub. ins (cubic inches)
*1 cub. yd = 0.768 cub. m.*
*1 cub. in. = 16.387 cub. cm*

## Capacity

1 bushel = 8 gals (gallons)
1 peck = 2 gals
1 gal. = 8 pts (pints)
*1 gal. = 4.546 L*

## Weight

1 ton = 2240lbs (pounds)
1cwt (hundredweight) = 112lbs
1 stone = 14lbs
1lb = 16oz (ounces)
*1lb = 0.454Kg*
*1 ton = 1.016 metric tonnes*

# Coal & Canals

Coal was known to exist within the Wigan area many centuries ago and was recognised as a valuable commodity by the fortunate owners of the land on which easily accessible deposits were to be found. The coal was used by the landowners as fuel for domestic heating and cooking, with any surplus being sold off to the neighbouring households.

A deed of sale dated 1350 relating to the transfer of a plot of land between one Margaret of Shuttleworth and Robert of Standish included a proviso 'to reserve the rights to fryston [fire stone] and secol [sea coal] if it is possible to find them in the lands mentioned'.

By the sixteenth century the mining of coal appears to have been carried out on a commercial basis, according to John Leland who wrote in 1538 of mining activities in the Haigh area: 'Mr Bradshau hath aplace called Hawe a myle from Wigan. He hath founde moche Canel like Se Coal in the grounds very profitable to hym.'

Mining as an industry expanded gradually over the years as demand for coal increased. However, the distribution of coal was restricted by the primitive transportation system available at the time. As a result the coal mines, cotton mills and other manufacturing industries would not expand by any significant degree until an economic and efficient method of moving coal from the supplier to the user had evolved.

The earliest method of distributing coal was via the system that had served the country's transportation requirements for centuries; namely by horses carrying panniers following the packhorse trails which traversed the hilltops linking the centres of population. However, by the start of the eighteenth century the movement of goods had increased to such an extent that a system of turnpike roads had begun to develop, enabling heavy and bulky items to be carted by large waggons pulled by horses.

The turnpike linking Wigan and Preston was established in 1726 and was maintained by the turnpike trust, a body of local land owners and merchants who collected money at toll booths from passing traffic and used it to maintain the road for the mutual benefit of the area. Unfortunately the increasing volume of heavy traffic, coupled with the fact that the turnpikes generally followed the low ground and were therefore susceptible to flooding, conspired to ensure that the roads were in a permanent state of disrepair. Tarmac was not yet available, and the crushed stone used to effect repairs was soon rendered useless by the traffic. Mr Arthur Young gave a graphic account of the condition of the Wigan–Preston turnpike during the eighteenth century in his book *Tour In The North Of England*:

> I know not in the whole range of language, terms sufficiently expressive to describe this infernal road. To look over a map and perceive that it is a principal one, not only to some towns but even to whole counties, one would naturally conclude it to be at least decent; but let me seriously caution all travellers who may accidentally purpose to travel this terrible country, to avoid it as they would the devil; for a thousand to one but they break their neck or limbs by overthrows, or breakings down. They will meet with ruts which actually measure four feet deep,

and floating with mud from a wet summer; what therefore must it be after winter? The only mending it in places it receives, is the tumbling some loose stones which serve no other purpose but jolting a carriage in the most intolerable manner. These are not merely opinions but facts, for I actually passed three carts broken down in these eighteen miles of execrable memory.

It became evident that the turnpike system would be unable to cope with the transportation of the vast tonnage of coal required to fuel the gathering pace of the industrial revolution and a number of progressive and forward thinking businessmen began to seek out a viable alternative.

Until 1803, when Trevithic's steam railway locomotive first breathed life, the only 'engine' available was the horse, and its limit of moving heavy loads over land had been tested and found wanting. However, it was known at this time that one horse could pull a load on water twenty times heavier than that which could be pulled by wheeled waggon over land.

During the 1730s the River Douglas was made navigable, by a combination of dredging and by the cutting of a series of new channels to remove bends, which enabled coal to be distributed from Wigan to various parts of the country by water.

Although this early experiment demonstrated the viability of transporting goods by waterway, few eighteenth-century entrepreneurs were willing to invest in such a speculative venture. However, attitudes were to change some thirty years later when the Duke of Bridgewater completed the country's first wholly man-made canal, which effectively halved the cost of coal to the city of Manchester.

## Lancaster – 1772

News of the success of the Duke's canal was not lost on the influential figures north of the Ribble who owned land which, although barren of coal, was rich in limestone. The Lancaster contingent were the most prominent in pushing for the installation of a canal, and over the next decade a series of meetings and discussions took place, with many gentlemen backing a proposal to access the coal south of the Ribble as cheaply as possible by cutting a canal between Lancaster and the proposed Leeds & Liverpool at Walton.

This proposal, whilst satisfying the immediate need for coal to be delivered to Lancaster, took no account of the vast tonnage of limestone locked in the hills around Kendal, and the ready made market for lime in the fields around Wigan. A persuasive argument was submitted to the interested parties in an effort to see the proposed line of the canal extended north as far as Kendal and south to Worsley.

> It is perhaps one of the most valuable lines for a Canal in the kingdom; as the country from Denham-Vale near Chorley, for some miles on each side of the proposed Canal at Worsley, are continued inexhaustible mines of the best coal, cannel, quarries of flags, and other rocks almost of every kind. At the other end from Lancaster to Kendal, is an immensity of the best lime-stone.

(Cannel, or candle, coal is of bituminous composition and is highly volatile, burning with a bright flame when ignited. Its light giving properties and readiness to burn made it a highly valued commodity.)

The promoters of the extension to the canal went on to list the valuable commodities which would be available if their proposal was acted upon.

> At Radlesworth, is a vein of fine flags, 6 yards thick, quantities are exported to Ireland.
>
> At Wheelton, is one of the best durable flag quarries, and most true bedded wallstone in the County.
>
> Whittle-Hills, and Hoghton-Tower quarries, are noted for good mill-stones many are exported to Ireland.

Also listed were the various coal seams around Chorley and Wigan: Mr Chadwick's – 9ft thick; Mr Norris's – 9ft thick; Mr Livesey's – 9ft thick; Standish – 16ft thick; Blackrod – 20ft thick; Arley 20ft thick; Haigh 46ft thick. The more rare seams of cannel are also recorded with beds 3ft thick at Haigh, Sir Thomas Gerrard's, and Mr Halliwell's.

A CURSORY
V I E W,
OF A PROPOSED
C A N A L:
FROM
Kendal, to the Duke of *Bridgewater*'s CANAL, Leading to the great Manufacturing Town of *Manchester*.
BY,
The several Towns of *Milnthrop*, *Lancaster*, *Garstang*, *Kirkham*, *Preston*, *Chorley*, *Wigan* and *Leigh*.
GIVING
A Particular ACCOUNT of the INTERNAL NATIVE PRODUCTIONS in the LINE.
TOGETHER
With the Advantages that will accrue to the PUBLIC.
ALSO,
Facts and Reasons, tending to shew that the CANAL proposed from *Lancaster*, to *Walton*, ought not to Terminate there.
AND
With several PROPOSALS addressed to the PROPRIETORS of the Grand CANAL, between *Leeds* and *Liverpool*, laying before them the MOTIVES that induced the *Lancashire* GENTLEMEN, to prefer the *Burnley* LINE to the *Padiham* LINE, and why it should not yet take PLACE, as there has lately been found a TRACT for the CANAL, by *Chorley*, to *Newborough*, which will be equally as near to *Liverpool*, by *Burnley*, as by *Padiham*: and with its Superior Advantages.

Front page of report promoting a canal to Kendal. (*Lancaster Ref. Lib.*)

There are above the coal and cannel vast quantities of bass, sufficient and proper to burn lime-stone; and also on the surface over the cannel, Haigh, for near 20 yards thick, a fine white rock, preferable to portland-stone.

It was estimated that the cost of cutting a canal 42ft wide at the top and 22ft wide at the bottom with a depth of 5ft and a length of 80 miles would be in the region of £200,000. To offset the initial capital outlay, it was envisaged that the proprietors of the canal would receive £30,000 each year in tolls. One ton of coal could be delivered to Preston for 6s 6d; Garstang for 7s 8d; Lancaster for 8s; and Kendal for 11s, with the price rising by some 2s to 3s for the more expensive cannel. A yard of flags could be delivered to Preston for 11d; Garstang for 1s; Lancaster for 1s 1d; and Kendal for 1s 3d. In the other direction, one ton of limestone could be delivered to Garstang for 1s 9d; Preston for 2s 8d; Chorley for 3s 6d; and Manchester for 5s 4d.

It was demonstrated that the carriage of merchandise and passengers by canal would be much cheaper than the equivalent journey over land:

> At this time carriage from Wigan to Kendal, is no less per tun, than £3. By a Canal 8s 9d.

The journey between Kendal and London by boat on the canal network was estimated to take six days and to cost 15s compared to the £3 5s which the faster, but also more

# The Old Tram Road

Old Lime Kiln at Preston.
Watercolour by George Shepheard 1770–1842. Dated 8th July 1819. (*Harris Museum*)

uncomfortable, stage-coach companies charged. A journey of 24 miles by post-chaise at the time would cost around £1 1s when the turnpike tolls were taken into account, whereas the equivalent distance travelled by canal would be a mere 10d.

> By a Canal, you not only travel cheaper than in a coach or post-chaise, but with more ease, safety, pleasure, certainty, and nearly as expeditious.

The arguments put forward for a canal to link Kendal with Wigan and thus to the ever growing network of waterways connecting the major industrial and economic centres of Britain proved to be irresistible. On 13 November 1771 at a meeting held at the Lancaster Town Hall a motion was passed to engage an engineer to survey a line between Kendal and the proposed line of the Leeds & Liverpool Canal at Eccleston. James Brindley, one of the country's foremost engineers was approached to survey the line and produce a cost estimate.

Unfortunately Brindley was unable to carry out the survey due to ill health and recommended that one of his pupils, Robert Whitworth, be appointed to complete the work. Mr Whitworth lost no time in embracing his allotted task and by 27 July 1772 was able to lay his proposals before the committee.

Unlike later road and rail engineers, the canal engineer's main consideration when deciding upon a new line was the flatness of the terrain, with directness of route being of much lesser importance. The installation of lockage on a canal would for evermore be the cause of disruption and lost time for the traffic using it and as such should be avoided where at all possible. If a few miles extra cut could eliminate the provision of lockage, this option was invariably taken. The other major factor which governed

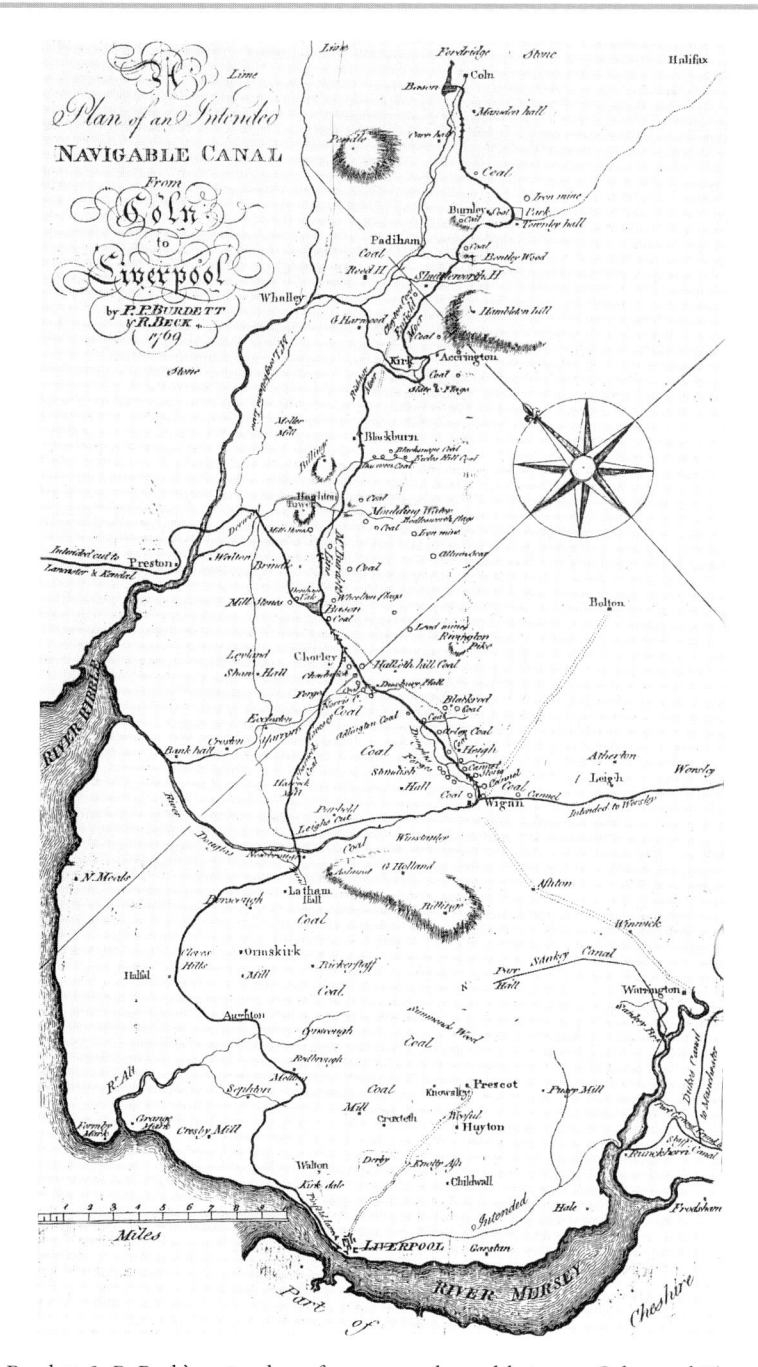

P. P. Burdett & R. Beck's 1769 plan of a proposed canal between Colne and Liverpool. The plan shows the intended cut to Lancaster and identifies the whereabouts of various mineral deposits. (*Lancaster Ref. Lib.*)

*The Old Tram Road*

the route was a political decision made by the company who determined through which general areas the canal should pass. The skill of the surveyor was often demonstrated in his ability to balance the volume of earth excavated with the amount of earth required for embankment.

Robert Whitworth surveyed a line unparalleled by any in the country at that time and proudly reported to the committee that 'upon this line there may be a level without the interruption of a single lock from Borwick to Liverpool, which will be a length of Eighty-six Miles this would be a much longer level than any that is yet laid out in England or perhaps ever will.'

His proposed line commenced at the Leeds & Liverpool Canal near Eccleston, crossed the Ribble below Penwortham old bridge, then headed west towards Kirkham and Barton and crossed the Lune near Skerton, a total of 54.5 miles on the level; at Tewitfield the canal was to lock up 86ft followed by 18 level miles to Kendal.

The canal was to measure 16ft wide at the bottom and 28ft wide at the surface of the water and to have a depth of 4ft 6ins.

Even at this early stage the crossing of the Ribble valley was highlighted as a massive expense when set against the remainder of the canal. The flood plain was to be crossed on embankment at a cost of £5,168 and the river itself was to be crossed by a brick built aqueduct of a sufficient height to allow the tallest vessels to pass under at high tide. The aqueduct was to carry a 12ft wide waterway and have an overall width of 36ft and comprise sixteen arches each 50ft wide. The cost of the structure was estimated to be £10,500. Although Robert Whitworth did propose an alternative cheaper method of crossing the river by providing 16ft of lockage either side of the Ribble thus reducing

Disused Lime Kiln at the junction of Fylde Road and Water Lane, Preston.
One of many sited along the route of the Canal and Tramroad. The limestone rock would be transhipped to the kiln where it was burned to a fine powder before being either spread across the fields or combined with sand to form mortar for building works. (*Harris Lib.*)

the cost of embankment to £1,978 and saving 1,960,000 bricks in the construction of the aqueduct which would result in a saving of £1,960. This saving was tempered by the additional cost of the lockage which, calculated at the rate of £60 per ft, came out at £1,920. The total cost of the canal connecting the Leeds & Liverpool with Lancaster (excluding the Lune Aqueduct) ended up at £85,089 or £81,859 depending on the level at which the Ribble valley was traversed.

Some committee members were dubious about Whitworth's proposal and he was asked to survey another, more direct, route omitting the westward detour to Kirkham. A line at a level 24ft higher was duly surveyed which worked out at the lesser cost of £78,340 or £75,110 again depending on the level at which the Ribble valley was negotiated.

Unfortunately the committee, when confronted by the enormous costs involved, suffered an attack of cold feet and resolved to abandon the project and shelve the plans. However, Mr Whitworth's efforts were not wasted and his early work was to form the basis for future engineers to develop a viable scheme for uniting Lancaster and Kendal with the coalfields of Wigan.

## *Twenty Years Later*

Almost two decades passed with little or no progress towards Lancaster's ultimate goal and the mood was one of frustration which was reflected in a paper written in 1791:

> With respect to Kendal, Lancaster, and perhaps Preston, it is now no longer a Question of Choice, but Necessity: either they must put themselves on a Footing with their Southern Neighbours, or submit to a Decline of their Trade and Population, and a Decrease in the Value of their Land, as a natural and inevitable Consequence: In short, a Canal is now become as necessary an Appendage to a Manufacturing and Commercial Town as a Turnpike Road.

On 8 June 1791, at the request of 29 prominent townsmen, the Mayor of Lancaster convened a meeting at the Town Hall with the aim of resurrecting and promoting a scheme for the provision of a canal. It was generally agreed by all present that a canal was essential to the future prosperity of the area and on the following day Samuel Gregson of Lancaster was appointed Clerk. Robert Dickinson and Richard Beck were engaged to investigate Whitworth's original line with the object of producing a shorter, more direct and cheaper route. However, Dickinson and Beck were unable to find a line better than Whitworth's, and in October John Rennie was approached and charged with the same task.

Rennie was one of the country's foremost engineers and he worked diligently during December and January to survey a more acceptable line.

Time was now at a premium. The Leeds & Liverpool consortium were proposing a line between Whittle le Woods and Wigan parallel to Rennie's, and if an Act of Parliament were to be granted for such a line then Lancaster would never have the direct access to the coal fields it so sorely needed.

Mindful of this possibility, the Lancaster consortium were spurred into action and

*The Old Tram Road*

a meeting was convened on 7 February 1792 with the object of drawing up a list of subscribers in order to apply for an Act of Parliament. Two weeks earlier Gregson prepared a report outlining the current position which he submitted to the interested parties for consideration. He began by reviewing the various proposals, which had been put forward during the preceding twenty years, before addressing the problem of crossing the Ribble valley:

> the next and most material object was passing Ribble – various trials were made to carry the Line on either side of Preston to cross the River to advantage, but the high land on one hand and breadth of the Valley on the other, baffled every attempt – two other objections arose – should the Ribble be crossed at an easier expence above Walton, the great River Darwent was afterwards to pass and would be attended with a very great expence – should it be crossed below Walton and not sufficiently low enough down the River, the Line would interfere with the private grounds of Sir H. Hoghton's Park, and continued by Within Trees (where it is upon the same Level as the Leeds Liverpool Line) to Clayton Green, which makes the Summit;

John Rennie (1761–1821)

Before Rennie commenced his survey, Gregson rode the full length of the proposed line on horseback in order to get a feel for the land it passed through. He wrote of his findings in glowing terms:

> previous to Mr Rennie beginning his Survey, Mr Jenkinson and myself were appointed to ride over the intended Line with him: The information I had before gained, strengthened by the observations made at this time, confirmed the opinion that this was the best Line for the CANAL, if sufficient Water could be obtained for the Lockage: (of which I shall make some observations before I close) – it not only leads through the very heart of the best COAL and CANNEL Country, but carries you through a Country full of Manufacturers, and full of inhabitants – a land that wants your Lime – a people that want your Imports – and as the Leeds Liverpool Line embraces the EAST and WEST, this Line at the same time that it carries you to your object, places you in the best probable situation (whenever it is found convenient) of uniting the NORTH and SOUTH.

Time was running out and a decision had to be made by the committee as to whether or not to commit themselves to the canal project. John Rennie was still carrying out his survey and could only give assurances of the viability of the canal and a rudimentary costing to help the committee with their decision;

8

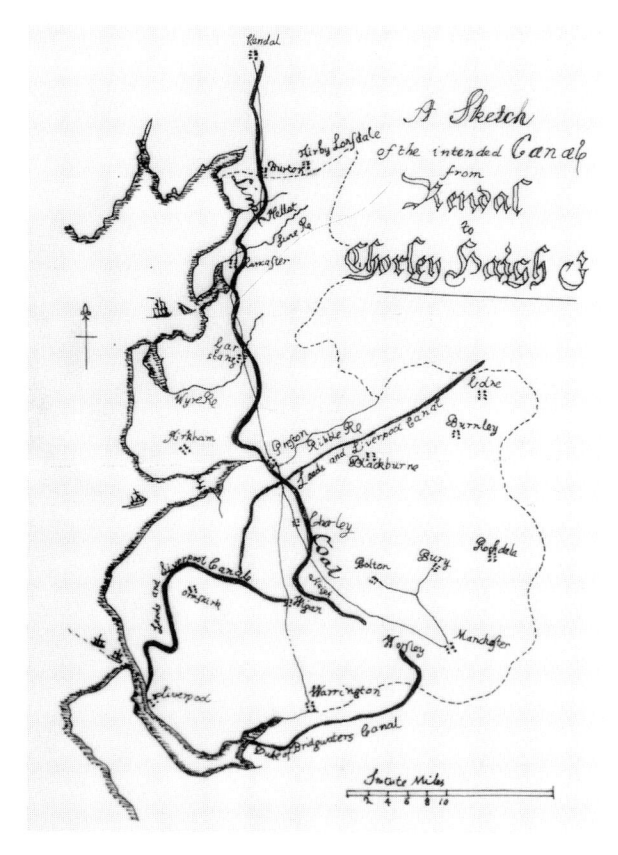

Mr Rennie has not finished his Survey, and most probably will not be able to compleat it before the Meeting. Of course he cannot make a regular Report or compleat an Estimate; but from the observations he has made, he is fully convinced of the practicability of the Line. That the Line South of Ribble (relative to the supply of which with Water, so many difficulties have been stated) may be fully and constantly supplied with Water, without injuring or interfering with the Mills or Streams already occupied, and that the whole will not cost more than £300,000 – how much less, it is not at present in his Power to ascertain.

Being well Assured of these particulars, and that no time should be lost in applying to Parliament, you have called a General Meeting, in order that the subscription may go forward with the Survey, and that both may be ready at the same time, which would not be the case if either was delayed.

Sketch map of the proposed route for the canal submitted to the Committee in 1792. (L.R.O.)

The savings in the cost of coal which canals brought to a region were well known by now. However, the savings in the cost of lime were perhaps less well publicised and Gregson sought to rectify this by estimating the potential savings which would be realised upon the canal's completion.

Based on delivery to a farm some ten miles from the kiln and a rate of use of 120 loads per acre, he estimated that by utilising one man driving two horses, lime could be supplied and delivered at a rate of £8 10s per acre whereas a similar exercise could be undertaken by canal for only £3 10s per acre. The tolls taken on the canal would directly benefit the canal proprietors and these were estimated to be £21,600 per year.

Gregson's arguments were sufficiently persuasive to carry the motion and by the end of the extraordinary general meeting the nettle had been grasped. The Lancaster Canal Committee resolved to make every effort to secure an Act of Parliament 'for making and maintaining a Navigable Canal from Kirby Kendal, in the County of Westmorland, to West Houghton, in the County Palatine of Lancaster'. Their labours were rewarded in June 1792 when the Act received royal assent incorporating the company and enabling the business of canal construction to begin in earnest.

## An Act of Parliament is Passed

The Act was to impose many constraints and conditions on the canal company, controlling the line and dimensions of the cut, the type and quality of goods to be carried, the rivers from which water could and could not be taken to supply the canal etc. The company would also be required to make provision to reinstate all land, roadways, waterways, drainage systems and buildings affected by the scheme and to construct sufficient bridges and aqueducts to maintain the quality of passage along river and road enjoyed previous to the canal being cut.

The financial constraints incorporated in the Act were to govern the amount and method of raising the money to complete the project and also to regulate the tolls to be charged to users of the canal.

The Lancaster and the Leeds & Liverpool Canals were destined to conflict with each other at some point between Wigan and the Ribble, and to ameliorate any future problems, the Lancaster Company was required to write to the Leeds & Liverpool asking that they set-out the proposed line and level of their canal, to enable the Lancaster to make sufficient provision to accommodate the Leeds & Liverpool, when constructed, with minimal disruption. The Leeds & Liverpool were required to set-out the said line within three months of the written notice being issued.

The width of the canal, including the cut, all embankments under 5ft high and cuttings less than 5ft deep, the towpaths, drainage and fences, was restricted to 30yds. This restriction did not apply to any docks, basins, or reservoirs necessary for the working of the canal.

The line was allowed a certain amount of scope for lateral movement to surmount any particular problems which may occur during construction but the Act demanded that the canal must not deviate from the proposed line by more than 100yds.

The depth of the cut was to be 7ft for its full length, and the size of the vessels requiring passage through the locks were to be 56ft long by 14ft wide. For the convenience of the canal users the company were instructed to erect stone distance markers every mile along the canal bank.

The company was restricted in the amount of tolls it could charge its customers:

for Tonnage and Wharfage upon Coal Navigation on the said intended Canal, any sum not exceeding One Penny Halfpenny per Ton per Mile: for Lime Stone, Salt Dres, Salt Rock, Bricks, Stone, Flags, Iron Stone, Coal Sleck, Black Bass, Iron Cinders, Gravel, Sand, Clay, Marl and Manure, any sum not exceeding One Halfpenny per Ton per Mile: for Lime, Pig Iron, Cast Iron, and Bar Iron, any sum not exceeding Two Pence per Ton per Mile.

Further rates were laid down for use of the lockage:

The said Company of Proprietors shall and may demand, recover, take, and receive for every

( 2515 )

## ANNO TRICESIMO SECUNDO

# Georgii III. Regis.

### CAP. CI.

An Act for making and maintaining a Navigable Canal from *Kirkby Kendal*, in the County of *Westmorland*, to *West Houghton*, in the County Palatine of *Lancaster*; and also a Navigable Branch from the said intended Canal at or near *Borwick*, to or near *Warton Cragg*; and also another Navigable Branch from, at, or near *Gale Moss*, by *Chorley*, to or near *Duxbury*, in the said County Palatine of *Lancaster*.

WHEREAS the making and maintaining a Navigable Canal for the Navigation of Boats, Barges, and other Vessels, from the Town of Kirkby Kendal, in the County of Westmorland, through the several Parishes of Kirkby Kendal, Heversham, Beetholme, and Burton, in the said County, and through the several Parishes of Warton, Bolton by the Sands, Halton, Lancaster, Cockerham, Garstang Church Town, Saint Michaels, Kirkham, Preston, Blackburn, Penwortham, *Preamble.*

Front page of the 1792 Act of Parliament for the Lancaster Canal. (*L.R.O.*)

## The Old Tram Road

Ton of Coals passing the Locks to be erected and set up on the said intended Canal, on the south side of the River Ribble, any sum not exceeding the sum of Two Shillings and Three Pence per Ton; but such Coals not to be charged with any further or other Duty than the said Two Shillings and Three Pence per Ton unless they shall pass more than eighteen miles North of Chorley, upon the said Canal.

Some goods were difficult to quantify by the ton and these were to be estimated as follows for the purposes of charging tolls:

Forty feet of round, or Fifty feet of Square Oak, Ash, or Elm Timber, and Fifty feet of Fir or Deal Balk, Poplar, Beech, or Birch, cut into Scantlings, and Fifty feet of Light Goods shall respectively be deemed rated, and estimated for One Ton weight.

Specific reference is made regarding the passage of the canal through Sir Henry Hoghton's land at Walton-le-Dale:

nothing herein contained shall extend, or be construed to extend, or impower the said Company of Proprietors to make the said cut of Canal in, through or on the East Side of a Certain Wood in Walton-le-Dale, in the said County of Lancaster, called Carr Wood, the property of Sir Henry Hoghton Baronet or deviate the same Cut or Canal through any of the Lands or Grounds of the same Sir Henry Hoghton, from the Course or Direction delineated in the said way or plan and set forth in the said book of reference without the Consent of the said Sir Henry Hoghton, his Heirs and Assigns, being first obtained in writing.

The authorised capital sum for the construction of the Lancaster Canal was £414,100 which was to be raised by issuing £100 shares, with £60,000 of the total being allocated to the Westmorland section and with the proviso that a further £200,000 could be raised if so required.

The company was charged to elect a committee at the first meeting consisting of 11 men, each owning 5 shares or more. Every committee member had one vote, with the chairman having the casting vote if so required. The officers to be appointed to run the affairs of the company were Treasurer, Receiver, Collector and Clerk.

The post of Clerk was awarded to Samuel Gregson who agreed to attend to the business of the company for £150 per annum with 10s 6d. allowed for horse hire and travelling expenses when required. He needed a local base to work from and rented a small office at the Judges Lodgings near Lancaster Castle for the weekly rent of 5s which included fuel for the fire to warm the office.

Gregson was to earn his keep during the ensuing years, as lack of money and a succession of disreputable contractors conspired to test his resolve to the limit. However, at the start of the project, he was no doubt filled with enthusiasm and optimism as he set about the task of organising the finances and engaging the professionals who would bring the project to fruition. John Rennie was installed as Principal Engineer for the works, with a salary of £600 per annum for which he was contracted to reside at Lancaster for five months of the year and attend the site as and when required for the remainder. William Crosley was appointed as Rennie's assistant and Archibald Miller as the Resident Engineer.

The Judges Lodgings, Lancaster.
Samuel Gregson administered the affairs of the Lancaster Canal Company from an office within. The building is now the Judges' Lodgings Museum. (S.B. – *1998*)

## Canal Construction on the Level

There were no large scale civil engineering construction firms in existence at the end of the eighteenth century, and although the cutting of the canal with its associated aqueducts, tunnels, cuttings and embankments was a major undertaking, the work was to be tackled by a number of 'small' outfits. This arrangement was far from satisfactory, with the engineer having to administer a number of small contracts simultaneously with inevitable delays, claims, counter claims and confusion.

Towards the end of 1792, John Pinkerton and John Murray were awarded the contract to construct the canal between Tewitfield, near Carnforth, and Ellel, near Galgate, and a lavish ceremony was arranged to commemorate the cutting of the first sod.

At first all went well, and Pinkerton and Murray were offered a further contract to extend the cut to Ray Lane near Caterall. Meanwhile the committee, ever mindful of the Leeds & Liverpool's desire to construct a canal along a line to the south of the Ribble on a similar course to the Lancaster, let the first contract for the South End between Bark Hill near Wigan and Nightingales near Chorley, to a third contractor, Paul Vickers of Thorne, in July 1793. (The canal between Preston and Kendal was referred to as the North End, whilst the length between Walton Summit and Wigan was known as the South End.)

Progress on the North End soon slowed, and Archibald Miller experienced endless

*The Old Tram Road*

problems due to inferior workmanship and unnecessary delays with Pinkerton and Murray. Matters came to a head in 1795 when Robert Whitworth had to be brought in as an independent arbitrator to resolve the differences between the client and the contractor. He concluded that Pinkerton and Murray were, by reason of their poor workmanship and their inability to progress the works at a reasonable rate, in breach of contract and they were summarily dismissed.

The canal company took over the contract themselves, employing their own labour under Archibald Miller's direct control, thus securing the future progress of the scheme, although by this time twelve months had already been lost.

> On Wednesday the 9th January, the committee of the Lancaster Canal, preceded by colours and a band of music, and attended by the diggers and a vast concourse of people, proceeded from the Canal Office to a place about a mile from the town where the first sod was cut. After several loud cheers it was taken up by George Suart Esq. (one of the committee) who made the labourers a handsome present. A great number of gentlemen dined at the White Hart; ale was given to the populace and the day was spent in festivities and rejoicing.
> 
> *Lancaster Guardian*

The South End of the canal was less troublesome in its construction and by July 1796 a sufficient length had been cut to allow traffic to generate a little sorely needed revenue.

During 1797 the Tewitfield to Preston section of the North End, which had been cut on the level, was complete except for the obstacle of the River Lune. Rennie proposed to cross the Lune with a brick built aqueduct 600ft long by 60ft high with five 70ft semi circular arches. His proposal was accepted by the committee with one amendment, which was to change the specification from bricks to the more traditional, although more expensive material, stone.

The company, no doubt recalling their earlier experiences of dealing with contracting outfits, decided to construct the Lune Aqueduct with their own labour force, again under the direct supervision of Archibald Miller. The construction of the foundations was by far the most difficult and dangerous part of the contract, and in January 1794 William Cartwright, who was later to feature prominently in the construction of the tramroad, was appointed to oversee the work. By July, 150 men were working on the site, and this massive work force, combined with Cartwright's dedication and determination to succeed, ensured that the foundations were completed by July 1795, whereupon the committee were moved to award him a silver cup in recognition of his efforts.

The remainder of the structure was duly completed for the total cost of £48,321, and on 22 November 1797 an armada of six boats sailed from Spitalls Moss, near Preston, to Tewitfield and back by way of an opening ceremony.

For the year 1797, John Rennie was paid a retainer of 250 guineas, with Archibald Miller acting as Resident Engineer being paid £400 and his assistant William Cartwright £250. The Clerk to the company, Samuel Gregson was paid £260 and the solicitor, Jackson Mason £300. The various land surveyors, superintendents and overlookers were paid between £35 and £100 each and the labourers were employed for 2s per day.

Archibald Miller was not retained by the company when his contract expired, and William Cartwright, who had already ably demonstrated his ability to the committee on the Lune Aqueduct, was promoted to Resident Engineer for the entire canal.

Under his driving influence construction work proceeded apace, stretching the company's financial reserves to the limit and by October 1798 he was able to report:

> I was at the south end of the Canal last week, and am happy to inform the committee that the trade on that part has very much increased since the Canal has been extended to Johnson's Hillock; but sorry to inform you that the road from Johnson's Hillock to the Turnpike Road in Whittle is in very bad repair, and may justly say impassable – I beg leave to observe to the Committee that if something is not immediately done for its reparation it will materially hurt the Trade on that end of the Navigation.

Whilst Cartwright reports the good news of his progress, this is tempered by his frustration at the condition of the roads along which he is forced to route all the canal traffic in the absence of a direct link to the North End of the canal.

1799 saw the canal earning a reasonable amount of income mainly from the packet boats plying between Preston and Lancaster, and the committee were able to record a revenue of £2,022 for the year. However, until the two ends were united, the earning capacity of the canal would be severely restricted, a fact foreseen by Gregson and mentioned in a letter to Rennie on 4 March 1798: 'I have no doubt if we get fairly to work on this Concern will do well, but it never will answer the desired purpose to either the publick or to the proprietors until we get over Ribble and communicate with the Coal Country.'

# A Tramroad is Proposed

There remained at the end of the eighteenth century four major natural obstacles to be overcome:

1. The rise in level of 76ft at Tewitfield, which required the construction of a flight of eight locks.
2. The Whittle Hills, near Chorley, which required the construction of a tunnel some 259yds long.
3. Hincaster Hill, near Milnthorpe, which also required the construction of a somewhat longer tunnel 378yds in length.
4. The most expensive article of crossing the River Ribble and its flood plane and the rise in level of 222ft to Walton Summit.

At the General Meeting of Proprietors held on the 2 July 1799 William Cartwright prepared a report with the aim of guiding the assembled gentlemen towards the most profitable use of their dwindling funds.

At that time, 52 miles of canal lay complete, with a further 26 miles yet to be cut. To the south, the completed section of canal which joined Bark Hill near Wigan to Johnson's Hillock, north of Chorley, cut through 12 miles of land rich in coal, and

# The Old Tram Road

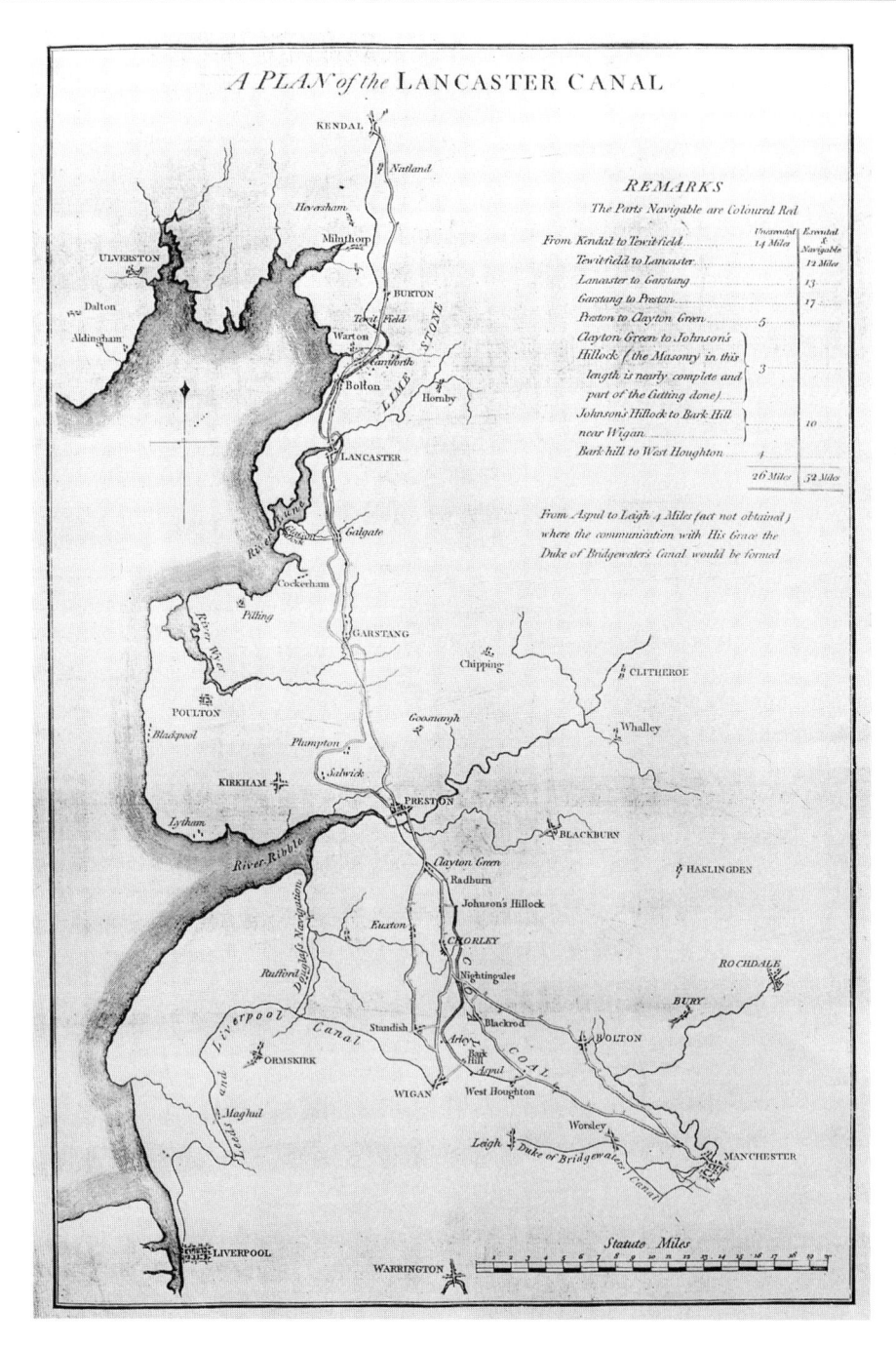

Plan submitted to the Committee by William Cartwright in 1799.
The plan lists the extent of works to date. (*P.R.O.*)

# A Tramroad is Proposed

Cartwright argued that it would be folly to progress the canal further south towards even greater deposits until an efficient system for transporting the coal to the country north of the Ribble had been established.

Preston was in need of some 20,000 tons of coal each year to fuel its burgeoning factories, and the other towns to the north wanted a further 20,000 tons. Their needs were ill met at excessive cost by the coalfields around Chorley from whence the coal had to be carted overland. The alternative was to buy coal at Wigan for transhipment via the Douglas Navigation, then across the Ribble at high tide to Preston Marsh where it was discharged and carted to the North End of the Lancaster Canal.

The South End of the canal was, to all intents and purposes, redundant due to the condition of the road at Johnson's Hillock: 'the road to the Navigation is hilly, narrow and in bad repair, and without great expence cannot be made capable of accommodating a great trade.'

Cartwright advocated that the very least that should be done was to continue the canal northwards to Radburn in Brindle where the roads were in a sufficiently good condition to enable the coal to continue its journey by land.

The original plan for uniting the two ends of the canal was to install a series of locks to lower the level from Walton Summit to the Ribble valley and then to cross the river via a stone built aqueduct. Cartwright estimated the expense of such an undertaking, together with the cost of extending the ends of the canal to the edge of the flood plane would be £180,945 plus the cost of purchasing water for the lockage. Realising the opportunity for completing the canal as originally envisaged had, for the time being passed, Cartwright went on to suggest a further, more realistic plan: 'I have turned my thoughts therefore to the forming of a junction by means of a double rail-road or waggon-way.'

The type of cargo to be carried and the topography of the land dictated that the two roads should follow separate routes between Penwortham and Walton Summit.

The north bound road (often referred to as the Coal Road, after the major cargo carried in that direction) would generally follow the natural fall of the ground, and descend the 215ft from Clayton Green to the southern edge of the Ribble valley, a distance of some 5037yds, at a rate of 6/10in. per yd. At Penwortham the steep 60ft decent into the valley would be effected by means of an inclined plane worked by a stationary steam winding engine situated at the top of the slope. The flood plane was to be traversed by means of a 7ft high embankment which would ensure that even the highest of floods would not disrupt the working of the road. A descent of 1/40in. per yd would allow an easy passage for the horses along the embankment to a substantial timber bridge spanning the river. Across the bridge, at Avenham, the ground rose steeply and here a second inclined plane and steam engine would be required to raise the waggons to the Lancaster level before continuing a level journey to the Preston Basin.

Cartwright calculated that the weight of materials to be carried by the south bound road (known as the Limestone Road), namely limestone, slates, paving stones and the like, would be greater than the weight of coal to be transported on the north bound

17

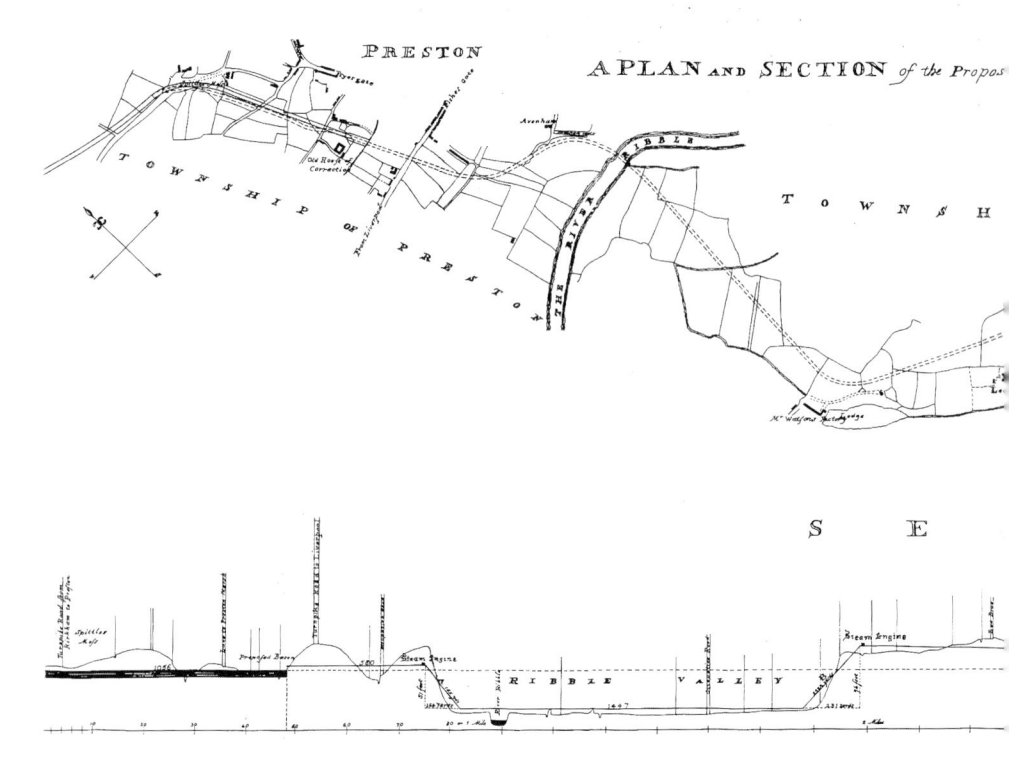

Plan and longitudinal section of the Tramroad prepared by William Cartwright in 1799. Rennie subsequently decided upon employing only three engines, and omitted the tunnel at the turnpike crossing. (P.R.O.)

route. In addition the south bound traffic would also have to tackle the considerable rise in level from the valley up to Walton Summit. In consideration of these facts, Cartwright tried to make the south bound journey as easy as possible by incorporated long level sections punctuated by short steep inclines worked by steam engine.

From the Preston Basin the south bound road gradually descended towards the Avenham incline, where the waggons would be lowered down the slope by the winding engine. There followed a nominal descent of a similar gradient across the embankment to the foot of the Penwortham Incline where the waggons would be hauled out of the valley. Three further level lengths of road together with three steam worked inclined planes brought the road up to the canal at Walton Summit.

The cost of the extension of the canal to meet the tramroad was estimated at £24,662 7s 6d. The cost of buying the land for, and constructing the tramroad, together with forming a commodious basin at Preston was expected to cost in the region of £34,902 12s 6d.

A large scale plan and longitudinal section of the rail road was left on deposit at the canal office for those gentlemen interested in viewing the finer details of the scheme.

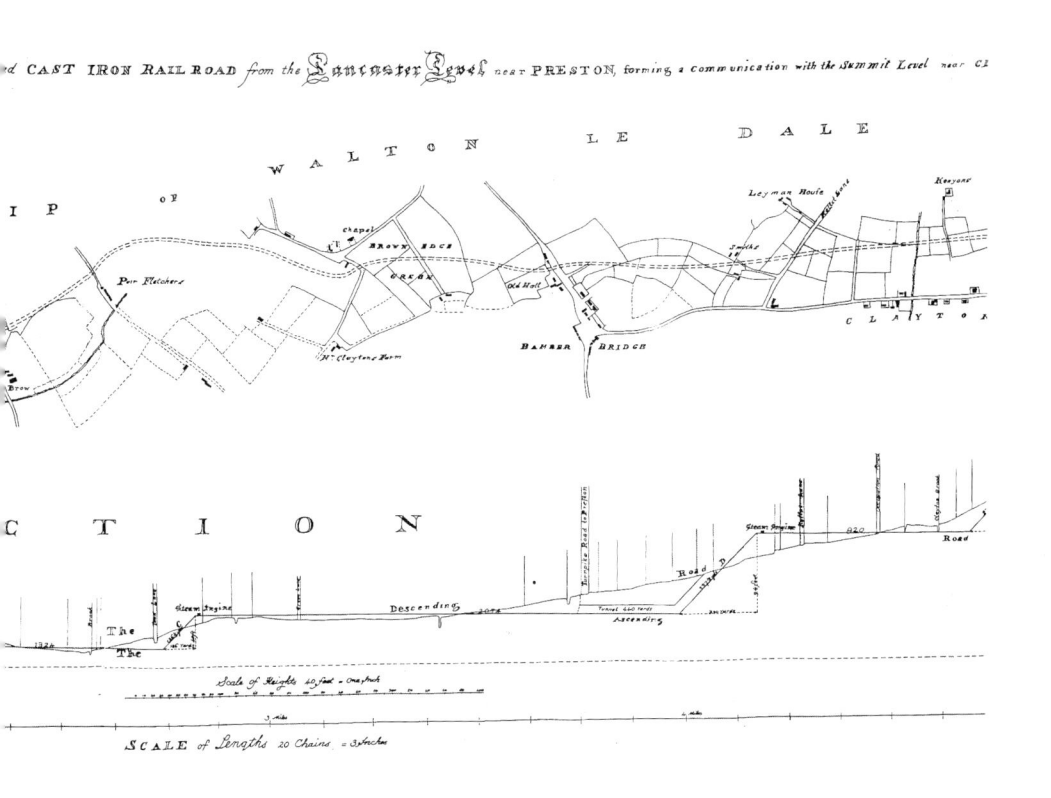

The size of the steam engine to work the various inclined planes was dependant on the degree of lift required. The engine serving the inclined plane with the greatest lift was to have a cylinder of 16 to 20ins in diameter which would cost £300. The engines serving the inclined planes at either side of the Ribble Valley were able to be of lesser proportions, as the descending waggons would act as a counterbalance effectively reducing the weight of the ascending waggons by two thirds. A typical engine was estimated to consume 8cwt of coal per day at 4½d per cwt and the cost of one man operating the engine 2s per day. When the interest charges on the purchase of the engine were added in, the daily running cost for one engine was found to be 7s 8d for which 300 tons could be drawn up the plane.

The waggons were to be 10cwt in weight, 6ft long by 4ft wide by 2ft deep with side boards. The main body was to be constructed of rolled iron and each waggon was designed to carry a load of 2 tons. Two horses were expected to pull six waggons fully laden with coal from Clayton Green to Preston and return with a load of limestone within 4 hours. The rails were to be 3ft long, of cast iron and laid with a gauge of 4ft 1½ins between the 'flanches'.

The committee were unable to agree on a course of action and it was resolved to consider the matter further at the next meeting of proprietors to be held in six months time. Cartwright's report and plan was circulated to the members for their perusal. It was at this juncture that rival factions sought to scupper the proposed tramroad.

## Opposition

The Lancaster and the Leeds & Liverpool Canal Companies were bitter rivals competing in the same market, and as such paid great attention to each others business with a view to gaining an advantage.

The Leeds & Liverpool Company looked on William Cartwright's proposal to unite the North and South Ends of the Lancaster Canal by means of a tramroad as a direct threat to their own trade.

Upon completion of the tramroad it was envisaged that the Leeds & Liverpool Canal, along with its associated coalfields, would no longer be required to supply and transport coal to the likes of Preston, Lancaster and Kendal. Similarly, limestone for use on the lands between Wigan and the Ribble would be supplied by the quarries of the Lancaster at the expense of the Leeds & Liverpool quarries.

The Leeds & Liverpool Company could not let this critical moment pass without making some attempt to counter its affect. To this end Mr James Monk, a committee member of the Leeds & Liverpool, wrote to Gregson on 4 January 1800 offering, what he termed, a less expensive proposal of mutual benefit to both companies.

Mr Monk proposed the cutting of a canal from the Douglas Navigation along the south side of, and parallel to the River Ribble to Penwortham followed by the navigation of the Ribble to a newly constructed basin on the north bank. From there he proposed half a mile of tramroad and inclined plane to link with the North End of the Lancaster Canal, with a view to replacing the short length of tramroad with canal and lockage as and when finances permitted. The cost of transporting 1 ton of coal by this route from collieries at Orrel and Dean to Penwortham was estimated at 4s.

Monk thought to press for acceptance of his proposal by threatening to undercut the Lancaster Company by supplying coal to Lancaster and Ulverston via the Douglas Navigation and the sea without any duty being charged.

On the 7 January 1800 the proprietors met and after a lengthy debate resolved:

> that it is highly necessary for the interest of this concern that the plan of the junction of the north and south parts of this Canal as delivered by Mr Cartwright or some similar plan should be adopted.

The resolution was not decisive and the proposal of Mr Monk was not altogether discounted.

Alex Haliburton, a proprietor of the Lancaster Company and owner of coalfields at Haigh, was not impressed by Monk's proposal and six weeks later wrote to George Clayton pointing out the pitfalls of the plan.

He interpreted Mr Monk's Scheme as a mischievous attempt to ensure the continuing

*Opposition*

prosperity of the coalfields and limestone quarries associated with the Leeds & Liverpool Canal which would be severely affected should the Lancaster Canal be united even if only by a tramroad.

Haliburton could see no benefit whatsoever to the Lancaster Company in Monk's scheme, indeed he estimated that Lancaster would loose £54,000 initially and £10,750 per annum for ever after if it were adopted. He further estimated that 1 ton of coal delivered to Lancaster by Mr Cartwright's plan would cost 12s 11d. whereas by Monk's plan the cost would be 16s 7d. In conclusion Haliburton asked Clayton to speak to as many members as possible before the next meeting urging them to disregard the proposal put forward by Monk.

Clayton must have been very persuasive for no more was heard of Mr Monk and his plan to abort the tramroad.

To finance construction of the tramroad, and the completion of the canal, an Act of Parliament was obtained on 20 June 1800 to raise an additional £200,000.

Even at this stage some committee members harboured grave doubts about the wisdom of building the tramroad and John Rennie and William Jessop were asked to prepare an alternative scheme.

In the event, it appears that a competition was organised and several schemes were prepared during May 1801. Rennie and Jessop proposed a stone aqueduct at a level of 40ft and a length of 640ft with three elliptical arches 116ft long. The height of the bridge from low water to the tow path was to be 57ft. Cartwright also proposed a stone aqueduct with three arches of 120ft span. A further scheme was submitted by Thomas Gibson who proposed a continuous aqueduct across the flood-plane, with three pointed arches spanning the river itself.

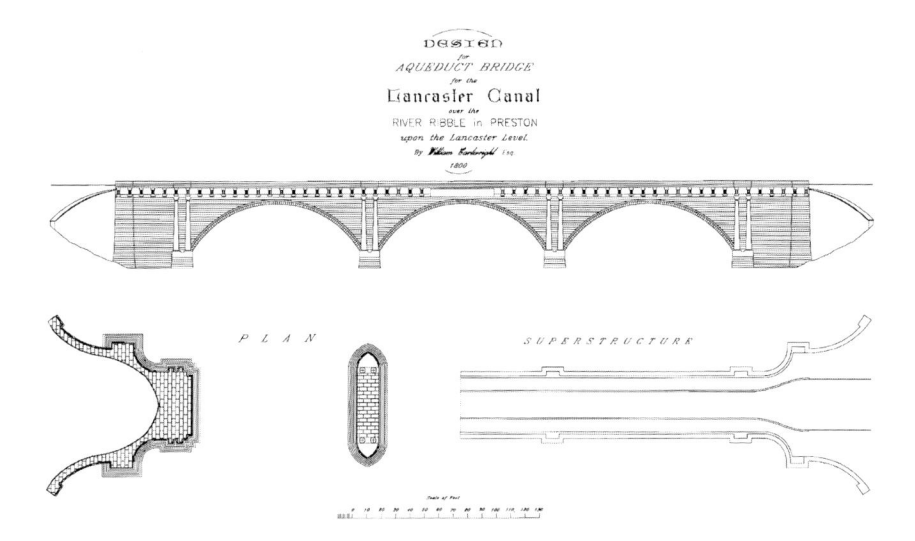

Design for an aqueduct over the River Ribble prepared by William Cartwright. One of three designs submitted to the committee for consideration in 1801. It was never built. (Based on drawing in *P.R.O.*)

After due consideration, the committee rejected all the proposals on the grounds of cost. This prompted Rennie and Jessop, concerned about the future prosperity of the canal, to put their weight behind the tramroad lobby and urged the company to adopt the tramroad as a short term solution to unite the canal. They warned the company that the tramroad should be looked on as no more than a temporary solution to enable the undertaking to generate enough cash to pay for the completion of the works as originally envisaged.

They simplified Cartwright's original scheme by proposing 4¾ miles of dual track laid on the one bed and following the Parliamentary line. The inclined planes at Kellet Lane and Todd Lane together with the tunnel at the Bamber Bridge turnpike were scrapped and the waggons were to be assisted up and down the inclined planes at Avenham, Carr Wood and Walton Summit by three static steam engines driving endless chains. Although the horses would, no doubt, have found Cartwright's tramroad preferable to work, Rennie and Jessop's scheme was considerably cheaper at £21,600, a fact that would have found much favour amongst the gentlemen of the committee.

The cheaper option was duly approved at a general meeting held on 7 March 1801 and three days later Gregson wrote to Rennie informing him of the decision:

> your report and Mr Jessop's was laid before the General Meeting of Proprietors held here on Tuesday. – It gave very general satisfaction. The resolution of the General meeting upon it is. – "That the Committee shall as expeditiously as may be, cause a Railway to be made to form a temporary communication between Clayton Green and the Canal at Preston, and that in executing the said railway the crossing upon the Lancaster Level should be kept in view so as to answer the necessary purposes of completing the Canal agreeably to the original plan.

At last, after years of argument and indecision, the tramroad was given the go ahead. William Jessop was paid £70 and John Rennie £112 for their advice, and William Cartwright was given the job of bringing the scheme to fruition.

## *Tramroads – Their Early Development*

Early forms of tramroads first made their appearance as part of the nation's transportation network over one hundred and fifty years before the cutting of the first canal. As with canals, the need to move coal was the main motivation behind their development.

In the early seventeenth century it was discovered that two parallel lines of sawn and shaped logs laid end to end would enable carts and waggons to run more smoothly and freely than over rough ground. In fact a single horse that could pull just seven hundredweight over land could pull forty two hundredweight along the primitive rails.

The coalfields of the North East saw the expansion of the 'new' form of transport, where a number of tramroads were established to move the coal to the rivers for subsequent distribution around the country.

Roger North, who on a trip to Newcastle observed this new mode of conveyance commented:

## Tramroads – Their Early Development

> When men have pieces of ground between the colliery and the river, they sell leave and lead coals over their ground, and so dear that the owner of a rood of ground will expect £20 per annum for the leave. The manner of the carriage is by laying rails of timber from the colliery down to the river, exactly straight and parallel, and bully carts are made with four rowlets fitting these rails, whereby the carriage is so easy, that one horse will draw down four or five chaldron of coals and immense benefit to the coal merchants.

As early as 1738 a report of an experiment involving the substitution of timber rails with cast iron, records that the experiment was not successful because the large waggons, in general use at the time, caused the iron rails to fail. It was some years before this problem was overcome by the simple expedient of building smaller waggons and linking them together to form a 'train', thus spreading the load imposed on the rails.

As with many new inventions and improvements, the iron rails were slow to catch on, and the timber rail remained in common use at least until 1765 when the following detailed description outlining the method of construction was penned.

> When the road has been traced at six feet in breadth, and when the declivities are fixed, an excavation is made of the breadth of the said road, more or less deep according as the levelling of the road requires. There afterwards arranged along the whole breadth of the excavation pieces of oak wood of the thickness of four, five, six and even eight inch square; these are placed across and at the distance of two or three feet from each other; these pieces need only be squared at their extremities, and upon these are fixed other pieces of wood well squared and sawed, of about six or seven inches breadth by five inches depth, with pegs of wood; its whole length; they are commonly placed at four feet distance from each other, which forms the interior breadth of the road.

However, the days of the all timber tramroad were numbered and it was only a matter of time before they were superseded by the cast iron rails which were rapidly gaining credibility as a reliable and more durable alternative. Many tramroad owners resisted the change, opting to wait for their original timber tracks to wear out and also for the technique of manufacturing iron rails to develop sufficiently to minimise the risk of investing large sums of money in wholesale replacement.

The mid eighteenth century saw many attempts to mass produce a reliable and cost effective cast iron rail. Robert Stephenson recalled an early experiment.

> I some years ago visited the great iron works at Colebrook Dale in Shropshire, where cast iron was indisputably first applied to the construction of bridges, and, according to the information which I have been able to obtain, it was there also railways of that material were first constructed. It appears from their books that between five and six tons of rails were cast on the 13 November 1767, as an experiment, on the suggestion of Mr Reynolds one of the partners.

The cutting of canals and the construction of horse operated tramroads went hand in glove. The canal provided a relatively inexpensive and reliable way of transporting large and bulky cargoes over great distances, whereas the tramroads distributed the goods from the wharves to the customer.

Where the topography allowed canals to be constructed on the level, the capital outlay was minimal. However, where natural obstacles such as hills, valleys or rivers were encountered the costs soared and in many instances became prohibitive. In such situations tramroads were to come into the reckoning as a possible alternative.

By the start of the nineteenth century popular opinion was embracing the idea of the increased use of tramroads, and in 1802 a Doctor Anderson in his publication 'Recreations in Agriculture' stated that:

> railroads might be established at a moderate expense in many difficult countries, that they would not cost near so much as canals; that they may be introduced in to districts where canals could not be formed, and that wherever surveys had been made for the latter it would be wise to examine the propriety of laying down rails instead of cutting canals.

During that year a committee from the Society of Arts conducted trials to assess the capabilities of horses pulling loads along rails and observed;

> a moderate sized horse with a descent of one in a hundred, carry, besides the wagon, 43 tons down and 7 tons up the incline chosen for the attempt.

## *The Construction of The Lancaster Canal Tramroad*

Towards the end of the eighteenth century, tramroads were being constructed using either edge rails or plate rails, with neither dominating and both having their advantages and disadvantages.

The edge rails, were of a 'T' shaped cross section and were more robust than the plate-rails. However, this design meant that only waggons with flanged wheels were able to run on the rails, which precluded their use elsewhere.

The plate rails, which were 'L' shaped and similar to angle iron in their design, were forever having the vertical flange damaged and were susceptible to gathering dirt and debris on the running surface. The main advantage of the plate-rail was that the waggon wheels had no flanges and as a consequence were free to be hauled along the highway where necessary.

William Jessop and Benjamin Outram were both partners in the Butterley Company and both gentlemen could be considered pioneers of the early cast iron rails.

In 1793 Jessop installed an edge rail at Loughborough, Leicestershire, and went on to propose a line at Little Eaton, Derbyshire which was subsequently constructed by Outram using plate-rails.

Outram is best known for his association with the horse drawn tramroad and, although he died in 1805 at the early age of 41, was responsible for the construction of numerous tramroads throughout the country, many of which outlived him by more than a century.

Arguably, his most famous tramroad was that constructed for the Peak Forest Canal Company which first came into service in 1799 and was in constant use until 1926. It was the Peak Forest that William Cartwright visited late in 1801 in order gain an appreciation of a working tramroad.

Outram published his observations and recommendations appertaining to the formation of tramroads in his *Minutes to be observed in the Construction of Railways:*

> the Sleepers or Blocks to fasten the rails upon ... should be of stone in all places where it can be obtained in Blocks of sufficient size; they should not be less than 8 nor more than 12 inches in thickness; and of such breadths, circular, square or triangular, as shall make them 150lbs. or 200lbs. weight each, their shape not material so that they have a flat bottom to rest upon, and a small portion of their upper surface level to form a firm bed for the end of the rails. In the centre of each Block must be drilled a hole one inch and a half in diameter and six inches in depth, to receive an Octagonal plug of dry Oak five inches in length, for it should not reach the bottom of the hole, nor should it be larger than so as to be put in easily and without much driving-for if too tight fitted it might when wet burst the stone. These plugs are each to receive an Iron spike or large Nail with a flat point and long head, adapted to fit the Countersunk Notches in the end of two rails, and thereby to fasten them down in the proper position. The rails should be of the stoutest Cast Iron one yard in length each, formed with a flanch on the inner edge two inches and a half high at the ends and three and a half in the centre, and shaped in the best manner to give strength to the rails and keep the wheels in the track. The soles of the rails for general purposes should not be less than four inches broad, and the thickness proportioned for the work they are intended for; on railways for heavy burthens, great use, and long duration, the rails should be very stout, weighing forty lbs., or in some cases nearly half an hundred weight each; for railways of less consequence less weight of metal will do-but it will not be prudent to use them of less than thirty lbs. weight each in any situation exposed to breakage above ground ... In fixing the Blocks and rails great attention is required to make them firm, and no earth or soft Materials are to be used between the Blocks and the bed of small stones or Gravel on which they rest. The rails must all be fixed by an Iron gauge to keep the sides at a regular distance or parallel to each other. The best width of road for general purposes is 4 feet 2ins between the Flanches of the rails, the wheels of the Carriages running in tracks about 4 feet 6 inches or under. Rails of particular forms are necessary where roads branch out from or intersect each other, and where Carriage Roads cross the Railways; and at turnings of the road great care is required to make them

William Jessop (1745–1814).

perfectly easy; the rails of that side forming the inner part of the Curve should be fixed a little lower than the other, and the rails should be set a little under the gauge so as to bring the side nearer together than in the straight parts; these deviations in level and width to be in proportion to the sharpness of the curve

In 1883 Clement Edwin Stretton published a paper to mark the eightieth anniversary of the completion of the tramroad. He implied that a bitter dispute raged between Jessop and Outram as to whether edge rails or plate-rails should be used on the Lancaster Canal Tramroad, and that Outram's plate-rail was chosen, much to the annoyance of Jessop. He also suggested that the name Outram was the derivation of the Old Tram Road.

Stretton's work has today been discredited and should not be taken as factual.

In actual fact, although Jessop is most associated with the fish bellied edge rail he also advocated the use of plate-rails where he thought appropriate and, in conjunction with William Cartwright, set about designing a plate rail suitable for the volume and type of traffic which the Lancaster Canal Tramroad would be subjected to.

Although similar to Outram's design, Jessop incorporated his fish belly concept to strengthen the horizontal element of the plate and whereas Outram thought one nail would be sufficient to fix his plate, Jessop advocated two.

In common with all the tramroads in use at the time, the length of Jessop's plate was to be 3ft with a cross sectional area of sufficient magnitude to support a 1 ton loading without detriment. This enabled a fully loaded waggon weighing some 4 tons with a wheel base not less than 3ft to be accommodated without any ill effects.

The 'L' shaped plates were to be cast of no. 1 pig iron not exceeding 40lb per yard in weight with a 3½in running surface, reinforced with a 1½in deep rib cast along the underside, and a ½ins thick flange 2in high at the ends bowing to 3in at the centre where the stress was greatest. The ends of the plate splayed out horizontally and 2 countersunk notches 3/8in × ½in were cast in, which formed 2 holes when butted up to an adjacent plate. The plates were fixed to stone sleepers by driving iron gad nails through the holes into oak pegs which were set into the sleepers.

Cartwright prepared the drawings and set the gauge at 4ft 3in. in his initial design but changed it to 4ft 1in before construction work began. The distance separating the north and south roads was fixed at 3ft 8in which would be sufficient to allow the waggons to pass each other without crushing any men or beasts who happened to find themselves between the two lines.

The entire roadbed was to be 24ft between the drains which would leave about 6ft either side of the dual track free for the halers to walk along and to allow the passage of workmen and unhitched horse.

The peace and tranquillity of Avenham and the Ribble valley was shattered with the start of the tramroad construction work, as over five hundred navigators descended upon the area. No doubt the good folk of Preston and Walton-le-Dale looked on the invasion of the navvies with some trepidation. They were a notoriously rough bunch of individuals given to frequent bouts of heavy drinking followed by outbreaks of violence either directed against themselves or at the local inhabitants. Some years

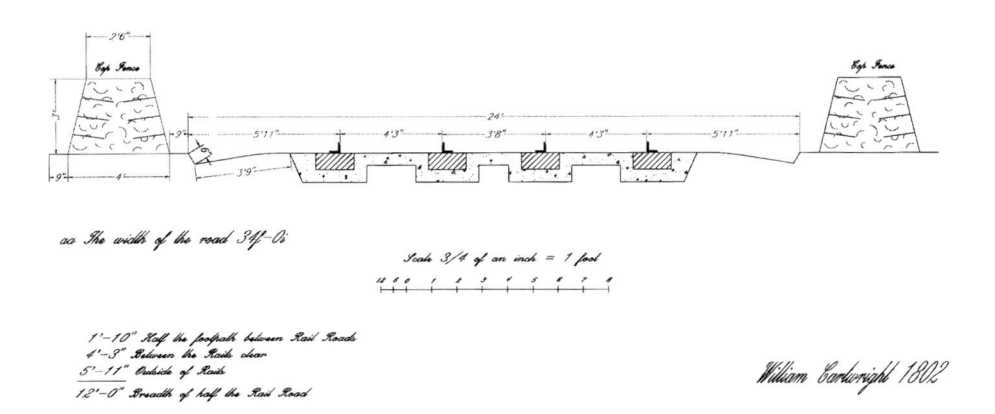

*Cross section through the Tramroad.*
It seems there was a last minute change of heart as to the width of the Tramroad. The distance between the rails was changed in pencil on the original drawing to 4′ 1″ and this was the dimension subsequently used in the construction. (Based on drawing in *P.R.O.*)

earlier the town of Chorley experienced their lawlessness at first hand and Gregson was compelled to write to the contractor urging them to keep their men in order:

> I am very sorry to be informed that some of your men have been behaving in a riotous and very illegal manner at Chorley. Such conduct will bring disgrace upon the works, as well as upon yourselves.

No doubt Preston was to witness many a fracas during the three years that the tramroad was under construction.

The navvies would have been drawn to Preston from all parts of the British Isles, with men from the northern counties predominating. A few would have travelled up from the south of the country in search of work and, as always, there would be a contingent of Irish and Scottish diggers. They took on the arduous career of professional excavator in order to guarantee a decent regular income to support their families back home, and were prepared to travel anywhere in the country in search of employment. With canal mania now at its height, the diggers were much sought after and consequently well paid. The Lancaster committee queried the 2s to 2s 6d per day wages that the company were paying the tramroad workers and Gregson was obliged to justify the reason for this in a letter dated 22 April 1802:

> As canal work is so very laborious, they must give such wages as will be the means of procuring and calling forth the utmost exertions of able Workmen; so that although the wages paid by the Contractors may be higher than for common Workmen in the adjoining country, yet when compared with the quantity of Work performed, it is by much the cheaper.

The navigator had developed the art of digging to such a degree that it was estimated that one man digging in good ground could excavate 12 cubic yards of earth during a typical ten hour shift. The diggers worked a six day week in all weathers and slept rough in whatever accommodation could be found local to the works. Each morning they would throw off their rudimentary blankets, pull on their boots and tuck into a breakfast of bread and porridge washed down by a flagon of ale. When sufficiently fortified, the old top coat was donned before setting off to walk to the site of that day's work. Some had their own spade with a blade honed razor sharp by the constant digging. Most used the spades, pick axes and wheelbarrows supplied by the contractor. The days work was long and hard and the navvies would rotate the laborious tasks of picking, digging and barrowing for variety, only stopping to rest for their dinner of bread and cheese and the inevitable ale. The afternoon would continue in the same vein under the watchful eye of the ganger man, and as darkness approached, if the company so required, bonfires would be lit to enable the men to work into the night. Normally the onset of darkness would signal the end of work for the day. The navvies would return their tools and set off back to their lodgings where they would prepare a meal of tatties and whey before setting out for the nearest tavern. After satiating the thirst brought on as a result of their labours they returned to their beds ready to re-enact the scene the following day.

Although the navvy formed the backbone of the work force, the successful progress of the works relied on the skill and accuracy of the land surveyor who set out the line and level of the tramroad. William Miller was employed in this position and his salary of £100 per annum reflected the importance of the post. A single miscalculation on the surveyor's part could cost the company thousands of pounds in abortive work. He would have been put under tremendous pressure during the construction of the tramroad with the various trades clamouring for his services to enable their work to continue unabated.

The two most influential figures concerned with the construction of the tramroad were William Cartwright and Samuel Gregson. Gregson provided the administrative expertise and Cartwright provided the engineering know-how. Together they were responsible for the day to day running of the contract, which caused them to correspond with each other at regular intervals. The letter books of the two gentlemen still exist and are held within the Public Record Office at Kew in London. A close scrutiny of the books reveals a fascinating chronological account of the trials and tribulations they encountered and overcame as they strove to unite the two ends of the truncated canal.

The earliest reference to the construction of the tramroad is contained in a letter from Cartwright to Gregson;.

## 19 June 1801 (*Cartwright to Gregson*)

'I must also beg leave to recommend two boats to be built near Radburn to carry free stone rubbish from Whittle Hills to form the Rail Road from Clayton Green to Preston" The boats were to be built to carry the spoil excavated from the tunnel to Penwortham where it was deposited in order to form the embankment across the Ribble Valley. It was thought that the boats could carry 20 waggons, each containing 2 tons of material.

The waggons were to be taken off at Walton Summit and hauled along the advancing tramroad to deposit their load at the head of the works.

The extension of the canal towards the Preston Basin was already underway: 'The cutting and works at Preston are going on very well.'

## 30 July 1801 (*Cartwright to the Committee*)

It was normal working practice during the cutting of canals to purchase the land, through which they were to pass, only weeks before the navvies were due to arrive. This was also true of the tramroad, and was the cause of its being held up on a number of occasions:

> I am now setting out the line to the south end of the Summit Level and the Rail Road to Bamber Bridge in order that the land may be agreed for which Mr Gregson comes over.
>
> The agreement with Mr Gorst should be immediately closed or the commissioners called out. This wholly stops the progress of the works at Preston, and will greatly delay the execution of the works at Fishergate Hill.

Cartwright foresaw the potential threat to the progress of the contract as a result of Mr Gorst's reticence to sign over his land, and although the canal company had the right by Act of Parliament to buy the land, if a price could not be agreed, the commissioners would have to be brought in to arbitrate. It was a requirement of the Act of Parliament that where disputes arose, independant commisioners were to be appointed who would listen to both sides of the arguement and then arrive at an impartial decision which would be binding on both parties.

## 8 September 1801 (*Cartwright to Gregson*)

> The works at Preston are nearly stopped for want of the agreement being executed with Mr Gorst.

## 16 October 1801 (*Cartwright to Gregson*)

William Cartwright visited the Peak Forest tramroad which had recently been installed by Benjamin Outram to his own specification:

> Whilst on my journey I went to see the rail road on the Peak Forest Canal – the rails, the waggons of the plan is very nearly the same which ours are intended to be – the rails are somewhat heavier and have not the flanch on the underside and only one nail hole at each end.

It can be seen that the Lancaster Company had already decided upon the design of rail to use, which although similar to Outram's in general appearance, differed in its detail.

Cartwright's visit to the Peak Forest did however, result in one major change to the tramroad. It had not previously been appreciated how great an area of land was necessary to effect a communion between canal and tramroad and it now appeared that the area available at Avenham would be insufficient:

> Upon considering the carrying of the navigation to the Ribbleside at Avenham I am of the

opinion that it will prove more desirable to continue the rail road from Avenham to the low ground purchased by the Company between Fishergate and Friargate.

Had Cartwright not undertaken his journey, the beauty of Avenham Park may have been lost forever. As the Preston Basin spawned a variety of industrial buildings and processes in its vicinity, no doubt a similar situation would have manifested itself amongst the rolling meadows which form the north bank of the Ribble.

## 9 November 1801 (*Gregson to the Committee*)

The line was surveyed, and sufficient land had been purchased to allow the tramroad contract to be let. Cartwright approached the contractors for a quote but was disappointed with the response: 'The forming of part of the Rail-way was not let on account of the Contractors requiring a greater price than Mr Cartwright thought it deserved.'

## 20 January 1802 (*Cartwright to Gregson*)

After lengthy negotiations, Cartwright finally accepted a price to construct a section of the tramroad: 'I have let the Coping and Forming of the rail road from Bamber Bridge to the south side of the Ribble valley and will begin of it next week.'

Throughout the early stages of the tramroad's construction, the acquisition of land posed a constant threat to its progress. The landowners were in no hurry to sell, whereas the canal company were anxious to see a deal struck as quickly as possible. Many landowners held out for a greater price, knowing that if the matter went to arbitration the delay would inevitably cost the company more money:

> The land in the Ribble Valley must be agreed for – but if the committee think it will be better to call out the Commissioner it should be done without loss of time.
>
> I have been with Mr Green who says Mr Knowles will not take less than £360 per Acre for the fields near Avenham, but has given me leave to rail the quantity we want off.

Mr Green accepted £150 for his land but Mr Knowles thought the offer of £315 made by the company for his plot was insufficient.

## 5 March 1802 (*Cartwright to Gregson*)

Although Cartwright thought Mr Knowles was being unreasonable in his demands, he decided to recommend that he be paid the extra £45 in order to avoid further delays.

The tramroad was to have a fence erected on either side of the road bed for its entire length in order to keep both people and animals from straying onto the track and also to prevent the navvies from destroying the surrounding fields during construction work. To this end the fences were to be erected in advance of the forming of the road bed. They were set up 25ft 6ins apart and were 3ft high, 4ft wide at the base and 2ft 6ins at the top. They comprised two lines of timber post and rail fence with quick thorn hedges growing between, referred to as a cop fence:

> I have begun to form the Rail Road from Clayton Green to the south side of the Ribble

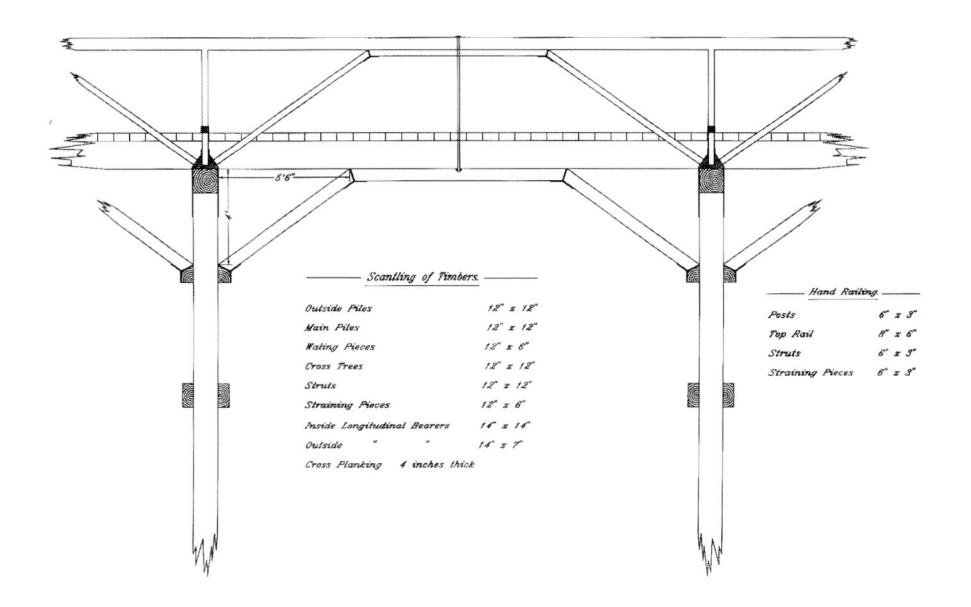

## The Construction of The Lancaster Canal Tramroad

Detail of a trestle bridge similar to the tram bridge but designed to carry a single track. (Based on drawing in *P.R.O.*)

Valley and expect to have the whole of the Cop fence finished in 3 months – 4000 feet of Deal Timber is purchased at Liverpool for the bridge over the Ribble and I shall begin to frame it in the course of a week.

This is one of the few references to the Old Tram Bridge; presumably the work went on without incident and as a result without comment. A drawing showing a timber bridge of the same design as the one over the Ribble but for only a single track shows the deck made up of 4in. thick planks fixed to 14in × 14in longitudinal bearers supported on 12in × 12in timber piles with bracing struts 12in × 6in The whole was fixed together with cast iron plates and brackets and a handrail was provided made up of 6in × 3in posts supporting an 8in × 6in timber rail rounded on the outside.

The bridge was to be no more than a temporary structure which would be demolished as soon as the canal earned enough revenue to commission the building of an aqueduct. It is testimony to the standards of workmanship of the period that even this temporary structure was constructed in such a thorough manner that it stood for 50 years before any major repairs were warranted.

## 20 March 1802 (*Gregson to the Committee*)

Rubble was being brought forward from the Whittle Hills tunnel excavation for use on the tramroad:

*The Old Tram Road*

The north side of the hill is Waggoning to form the Basins and inclined plane – the Basins are set out and for the present the sides are cambered up with sods, I think the form of them will be found very convenient, and they are capable of extension – Land is purchased for that purpose.

The tramroad was being advanced either side of the Ribble:

'The forming the Rail Road and the making the Cop fencing is proceeding all the way from the Summit mainly to the edge of the Ribble Valley. On the north side of Ribble the Rail way is joining to Avenham Walk.'

The purchase of land in the Ribble valley was still proving troublesome and Cartwright urged the committee to take all reasonable steps to close the deals quickly:

It is very necessary that the embankment across the valley should be proceeded with and Mr Cartwright desires that no time may be lost in permitting him to set men in, this will be the latest part of the whole works.

## 23 March 1802 (*Cartwright to Gregson*)

One of the landowners concerned was a Mr Norris who owned the Penwortham Factory situated at the bottom of Factory Lane, now owned by Vernon's Ltd. One acre of his land was needed, and Cartwright made his first approach to a Mr Watson who was one of six tenants at the factory.

I waited on Mr Watson with one of the Canal Acts who informed me that Mr Norris was very much displeased with the idea of the Canal Company making a Rail Road instead of a Canal, and erecting a Steam Engine on his land which he thought their act did not authorise them to do. I am afraid Mr Watson is inclined to be troublesome, and if the Committee call out the Commissioner. It will be necessary to include Mr Norris's Land.

It appears that even at this stage many of the locals were expecting a canal to pass through their lands and seemed a bit put out when the canal company began constructing a tramroad instead. Mr Norris raised the first objection, of which there were to be many, about the stationary steam engine and associated reservoirs being constructed at the top of the Penwortham Incline. Cartwright was becoming impatient with the constant wrangling and urged the committee to make a decision:

It is very necessary for the Committee to make a determination respecting the land in the Ribble Valley for if it is not immediately purchased I shall not have employment for the men and it is far behind the other part of the work.

## 30 March 1802 (*Gregson to Cartwright*)

The iron plates for the splice roads, or sidings, were manufactured in small quantities at a local iron works: 'Two hundred yards of rails are come from Halton one half went by the Packet this morning and the other will be sent tomorrow.' As for the main line, it was thought that local companies would be unable to meet the demand and it was decided to advertise the contract for the supply of good quality rails nationally.

In preparing the advertisement, Gregson sought clarification from Cartwright as to the exact wording of the specification:

> I understand that the No. of pig iron is not always the same, for instance the No. 1 best pig which is cast at one foundry may only be equal to No. 2 at another – it may therefore be well to explain your mission by adding after No. 1 "that is from iron of the most approved quality for work of this nature" without any mixture etc.
>
> I presume from the appearance of the rails when cast you cannot form a judgement of the metal or mixture which may have been made use of and as you fix them to be delivered to bear a certain weight it is the last check which you can have upon the metal without describing it further.

## 1 April 1802 (*Gregson to Cartwright*)

In writing the specification for the iron plates, Cartwright appears to have been undecided as to what weight they were to carry and Gregson, who was already being asked for details by prospective tenderers needed a decision:

> I have had some applications for the specification of the Rails, must the blank for the weight they are to carry be filled with *two Tons*? do not fail to give me an answer by return of the mail.

Presumably Cartwright ultimately settled on 5 tons, for this was the weight specified in subsequent orders.

Unfortunately there were no British Standards at that time and Gregson toiled with the wording of the specification in an effort to ensure that all the various ironworks tendered on the same basis to provide the quality of rails needed. Gregson's efforts were to prove in vain and over the coming months the problems of obtaining good quality rails in the quantity required were to dominate the proceedings.

The Lancaster Gazette ran Gregson's advertisement on the 3 April 1802

## April 1802 (*Gregson to Thompson & Hazeldene*)

Shortly after the advertisements appeared, a number of ironworks based in Wales, Shropshire and Yorkshire expressed an interest, and specifications were sent to Thomson & Hazledene, Sturges & Co., Cragg, Bateman & Sharratt at the Salford Ironworks, Mr Richard Wright of West Bromwich near Birmingham, W & J Rigby, The Aberdare Iron Co., Grazebrook & Whitch and Ayden &

---

**TO IRON FOUNDERS**

The Lancaster Canal Company are ready to receive proposals from any person or persons who are willing to contract for the delivery of a quantity of CAST-IRON RAILS, for a ROAD, about four miles in length, The rails are to be delivered by the contractors upon the works, at or near Preston, in the county of Lancaster. – The specification with a drawing of the rails, and any other information, may be had by applying to Mr. GREGSON at the Canal-Office, Lancaster; or to Mr. CARTWRIGHT, engineer, Preston. *§* The proposals must be delivered at the Canal-Office, Lancaster on or before the 18th day of April, 1802.

Elwell. Thompson & Hazledene asked Gregson whether he knew the cost of transhipping the rails: 'I am not acquainted with the freight charged from Preston Brook to Liverpool – From Liverpool to Preston I apprehend the freight would be 6s 8d per Ton.'

## April 1802 (*Gregson to Broomfield & Co.*)

Apparently some of the ironworks offered to tranship the rails to Liverpool only, and Gregson made enquiries as to the cost of getting them to Preston via the Leeds & Liverpool canal and the Douglas Navigation.

> The Lancaster Canal Company are about making Contracts for a quantity of Cast Iron Rails to the amount of 400 or 500 Tons – it is probable a portion of them may come out of Shropshire or Wales and be delivered at Liverpool – I take the liberty of requesting you will favour me with the cost of putting the rails on board the Boats in the Canal and the freight and their charges upon them supposing yourselves or any other person were to engage to deliver them at Preston.

## 13 April 1802 (*Committee decision*)

The ironworks offering the lowest price were contracted to supply the bulk of the rails, a decision which in the long run would cost the canal company dear:

> The various proposals for furnishing the cast iron rails were taken into consideration, where it appeared that the proposals of the Aberdare Iron Company were the lowest.
>
> Ordered that Mr John Scales on behalf of the Aberdare Iron Company be agreed with the delivery of three hundred Tons of Cast Iron Rails at Preston at the price of Ten Pound Ten Shillings per Ton – and that a reserve of a further one hundred Tons be made at the same price, provided they may expect the 300 Tons to the satisfaction of the Committee.

## 22 April 1802 (*Gregson to Cartwright*)

The second lowest tender was also accepted and an order for 100 tons was placed. Gregson asked Cartwright to arrange for the company's carpenter to carve a timber replica of the rail in order for the ironworks to prepare their moulds:

> I have received a letter from Messrs Ayden & Elwell of Shelf Iron Works near Bradford saying that they will execute our Rails at £10 15s per Ton laid down on the work – would you have Mr Dickinson to make a pattern rail *exactly* the same as the one sent to the Aberdare Iron Works.

## April 1802 (*Gregson to Messrs. Ayden & Elwell*)

Gregson wrote to Ayden & Elwell to arrange for the execution of the formal contract and also to ask for an address to which the pattern rail should be delivered:

> I have received your favour informing me that you agree to furnish the Cast Iron Rails at £10 15s per Ton delivered at Preston.
>
> Our Committee will meet on Friday the 30th inst. when an agreement will be made out and sent for your signatures, in the meantime the pattern Rail shall be got made.

Please to give me a line by return of post saying where the pattern Rail must be directed to be left *in Bradford* – I am afraid carriers may be careless about it, except there is some place named for its being left at.

## 29 April 1802 (*Cartwright to Gregson*)

Meanwhile back at Walton Summit, progress was being made:

The Basin at the north-end of your Summit Level is mainly made and the inclined plane is forming, it is therefore absolutely necessary for you to give directions for the small engine to be made, and the chain for the inclined plane.

## 1 May 1802 (*Gregson to Messrs. Ayden & Elwell*)

After receiving precise directions from the ironworks, Gregson dispatched the pattern rail:

The pattern Rail was sent off by the Skipton waggon this day directed for you to be left at the Cock Inn, Halifax – this rail is made a little longer than the Specification describes, in order to allow for the contraction of the metal in casting – when cast the rails should be 3 feet long.

The rails were to be delivered to the works and Gregson gave detailed directions:

We must beg of you to use every exertion to furnish us with as many rails as you possibly can in the first two months, you will please write to Mr Cartwright, Engineer, Preston as soon as you forward any part of the rails, and you will desire the person with whom you have contracted for the cartage to write to Mr Cartwright and inform him the day on which he will bring the first load – he must come thro' the Town of *Brindle* and Mr Cartwright will send a person to meet him there and conduct him to the place where they are to be laid down – this plan will save him from 3 to 4 miles of cartage and the expence of going thro' one Turnpike Bar.

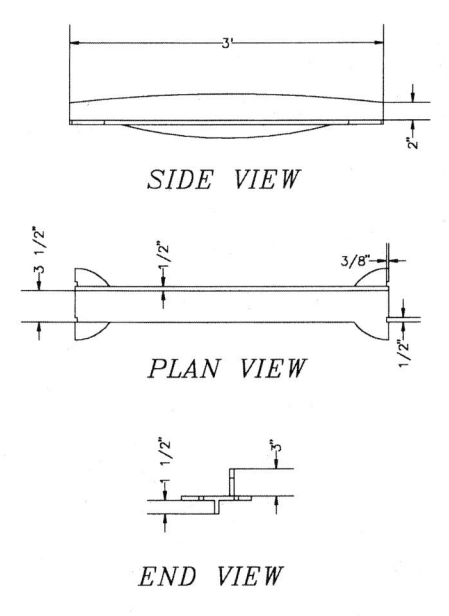

*SIDE VIEW*

*PLAN VIEW*

*END VIEW*

Typical detail of a plate rail.
The vertical flange is deeper at its centre where the stresses are greatest. A rib is cast to the underside to support the horizontal running section. The two notches cast into each end form square holes when butted to an adjacent rail through which the plates could be spiked to the sleeper. (S.B.)

## June 1802 (*Gregson to John Scale, Aberdare Iron Co.*)

The Aberdare Iron Company intended to ship their iron rails from Wales direct into Preston via the River Ribble. Gregson was worried that if this plan were carried through, the consignment may never arrive:

> I observe that you mention that you intend to send a vessel of from 45 to 50 Tons with the rails to Preston. I think it necessary for your information to say that the vessel should not draw more than 5 feet 6 inches water to get up the river to Preston.

He went on to point out that normally, only boats with a displacement of 4ft 6ins could be accommodated by the silt filled Ribble. To obviate a potential calamity Gregson suggested that the iron rails be shipped to Lancaster where the Lune offered a safer passage. From there, the plates could be shipped by canal barge to Preston. He even offered to wave the duty for the use of the canal.

## 9 August 1802 (*Gregson to Scale*)

Two months later the Aberdare Company had failed to deliver a single rail and Gregson expressed his disappointment:

> The Lancaster Canal Committee are extremely hurt that they should have occasioned to observe that you have paid little attention to your Contract with them. It is a matter of serious consequence to their works that the rails should have been delivered agreeable to the Contract – they have been under the necessity of ordering a quantity to be cast at an additional price and until you begin to deliver regularly, that order must be continued, and they must look upon you for making good the extra expence they are put to. They trust that no further time will be lost on your part.

## 16 August 1802 (*Gregson to Cartwright*)

The Aberdare Company replied with what appears to be a stalling tactic, and Gregson broke the news to Cartwright:

> I have received a letter from Mr Scale this post saying that he has 80 Tons rails ready but cannot get a vessel to go to Preston – he has sent to engage one to come to Lancaster, and I hope he will not meet with any further difficulty.

## 10 September 1802 (*Gregson to Scale*)

A further month was lost and there was still no sign of the rails from Aberdare, supposedly due to the problems encountered in finding a suitable vessel. Gregson, in frustration, contacted Mr Scale of the Aberdare and informed him that, had he known at the time of letting the contract that shipping the rails would be such a great problem he would have let the contract to ironworks in the locality of the tramroad.

## 28 September 1802 (*Gregson to Aydon & Elwell*)

The other ironworks contracted to supply the rails were performing admirably and

Gregson paid for the first batch."Mr Cartwright has forwarded your Bill for the iron rails delivered amount = £297 1s 0d for which sum I enclose a Draft."

To compensate for the deficiencies of the Aberdare Company, Gregson lent on the more responsive Yorkshire firm to try and make up the shortfall."The Canal Committee will be much obliged by you using every exertion to give them an additional quantity of rails as soon as possible"

## 1 October 1802 (*Gregson to Cartwright*)

At last the rails from Aberdare were dispatched: 'I have a letter from Aberdare saying that on the 19 September a vessel sailed with 3139 plates.'

## 6 October 1802 (*Gregson to Cartwright*)

Meanwhile, at the tramroad, the steam engine at the Penwortham incline was being modified: 'A few of the Committee have been together this morning and wish you to close the agreement with Mr Watson subject to the Horizontal Flue being made in the manner you state.' Cartwright was authorised to pay Mr Watson £200 per acre which Gregson hoped would not affect the delicate negotiations continuing with Sir Henry Hoghton.

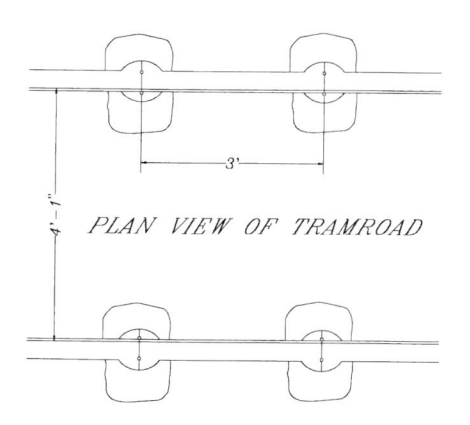

Plan View of Tramroad. (S.B.)

## 10 October 1802 (*Gregson to Aberdare Iron*)

Gregson acknowledged Mr Scales notification of the dispatch of the plates:

> Your favour I have received informing me that the Prosperity sailed on 19 September with 39½ Tons of Plates and that you were shipping 65 Tons at Neath which would sail about the 25 September. Both these vessels are consigned to Liverpool and the Rails to be forwarded from there.

He went on to inform Mr Scales that he would not hold his breath until the plates arrived and for good measure had a dig about the time that the company had been kept waiting:

> I shall decline looking out for any vessel here as it does not appear that you can fix any given time for having a quantity ready.
> We have about 3 miles of the road ready for the rails, and we have lost a very fine season for laying them.

## 11 October 1802 (*Cartwright to Gregson*)

Three weeks after setting out from South Wales the Prosperity made it into Liverpool and William Cartwright went over to inspect the rails as they were unloaded:

> This morning I went down to Broomfield's Wharf, about 10 Tons of Iron Rails from Aberdare was unloading and I believe 30 Tons more are in the river in which will be kept to night – I am very sorry to send you a sample. I confess if they had been moulded in Gravel instead of Sand they could not be rougher handled and the metal of itself is the worst I ever saw a specimen I send you to lay before the committee.

The appearance of the metal was not the only problem:

> I took two of the rails up to our workshop and broke them with a weight = to 3½ Tons on the lever, I therefore cannot recommend to the Gentlemen of the Committee to make use of any of those rails for I really don't think they will answer the purpose.

The rails already supplied by Aydon & Elwell were of much better quality:

> The rails got from Shelf Iron Works are exceedingly good metal and well executed and on trial I found them to break with exactly 6 Tons – their rails weighing 40lb and the Aberdare mainly 48lb.

Cartwright went on to recommend that the load from Aberdare be rejected and that two or three local foundries should immediately be contracted to supply 70 or 80 tons of rails each although he accepted that the company would have to pay between £12 and £12 10s per ton for them.

## 13 October 1802 (*Committee Meeting*)

The committee were informed of the Aberdare consignment and instructed the company solicitor to act on their behalf:

> Mr Cartwrights report was read stating that he had received part of the Cast Iron Rails from the Aberdare Company: that upon trial being made upon two of the rails they broke with a weight equal to 3½ Tons, that they were very bad castings and were each 3lb heavier than the Contract.
> Ordered that Mr Mason write to the Aberdare Iron Company: and inform them that the rails are not delivered according to the Contract and that they will not be accepted.

## 13 October 1802 (*J. Mason to Aberdare Iron*)

Mr Mason lost no time in drafting a suitably scathing letter and fired it off to Wales:

> I am directed by the Gentlemen of the Lancaster Canal Committee to inform you that Mr Cartwright their Engineer has reported to them that he has received a part of the cast iron railway from your Aberdare Iron Works and that he had tried some of the rails which broke with a weight equal to 3½ Tons that they are very bad castings, of very inferior metal and are 3 pounds heavier than the Contract weight and therefore, as the rails in every respect contrary to your agreement. They will not accept of them, and they are now laying at Liverpool

at your risk. – I have further to add that what with the delay in sending the Iron Rails, and the disappointment in finding them unserviceable when they are come, great damage has been sustained by the Company; for which an adequate compensation will be expected, and I require your immediate answer

## 15 October 1802 (*Gregson to Cartwright*)

The tramroad was falling further and further behind programme as a result of the Aberdare fiasco and Gregson's letter to Cartwright contained a hint of despair:

> It is very unfortunate that these rails should turn out so bad – it will throw the works very much behind the time we have held out for their completion, and I am at a loss to advise what steps should be taken in the business – we cannot order from other houses until a total stop is put upon the castings from Wales.

## 20 October 1802 (*Cartwright to Gregson*)

Nine days had passed since the Aberdare rails were rejected and Cartwright was becoming impatient with the committee who were not forthcoming with any decisions as to how the matter should be addressed:

> I hope the Gentlemen of the Committee will soon come to some resolution respecting the iron rails, we are now *loosing time* the Road being all formed long ago and awaiting for iron

He suggested that as well as the supplies from Ayden & Elwell, orders should be placed with two local foundries:

> Pig iron is now at a lower price than at the time of the Contract with Mr Scale. I hope the Halton Iron Company can now afford to lay down iron rails at Preston for £12 – 10s per Ton – I can get about 4 or 5 Tons per week cast here at that price and if the Halton Iron Company could lay us down twice that quantity it will be putting us forward with the quantity we get from Yorkshire, so that the Road may be finished in some reasonable time.

Meanwhile the tunnel under Fishergate was underway but the navvies were hampered by the ingress of groundwater:

> The heading at Preston goes on but slowly having only one end that men can work at having not succeeded in getting down the other part and I am afraid we shall not be able to accomplish it without the aid of a small engine, the 6 horse engine which is making for the inclined plane at Walton Summit will answer this purpose, as the trade may be carried on for some time after the Rail Road is done without the engine by making use of the splice roads.

The splice roads served the outer arms of the Summit Basin and offered an easier gradient than the inclined plane which allowed horses to haul the waggons without the aid of an engine.

> The large engine should now be ordered – I am informed that the Committee may be best and cheapest supplied with cylinder and boxes and all the heavy articles for this engine from Mr Wilkinson's works near Wrexham. I believe their prices are much lower than at the Low

*The Old Tram Road*

Moor Iron Works. Boulton and Watt get all their cylinders made at these works. If the Committee will authorise me to give the order I shall take pleasure in doing it.

The three engines for the inclined planes were described as small in an estimate prepared only five weeks later and were supplied by a firm called Summerfield and Atkinson. Therefore I would presume that the large engine to which Cartwright referred was the 70 horse power engine which was needed to pump water from the Ribble to supply the canal.

The contract for the supply of the stone sleepers was proving unsatisfactory and Cartwright proposed a change of policy:

> The rail road stones White is preparing are too large, the size should not exceed from 16 to 20 inches long – 12 inches broad and from 8 to 10 inches thick – the stones bored are not well done – I wish them to be sent here unbored. I can get them done here for about half the price that is given at Lancaster.

On a personal note Cartwright asked the company to sell him some land to build a house on:

> I have just received a notice to quit my house, the person who lately purchased it wishes to come to it himself – I know of no other House in Preston that I can take – consequently shall be under necessity of building a house. There is a small piece of ground near the Play House, that will exactly answer my purpose – I therefore beg the committee will please to grant me a lease of it forever at the yearly value of what it cost them – I shall esteem it a

Stone Sleeper.
Note how the impression of the plate ends have been worn into the stone. Seventy years of heavy traffic has taken its toll, and the two adjacent plates have worn the stone unevenly. Towards the end of its life the Tramroad must have been very noisy with each wheel of each waggon clanking over a badly aligned joint every 3 ft. of its five mile journey. (S.B. – 1998)

## The Construction of The Lancaster Canal Tramroad

The Theatre Royal.
Painted in 1854 by J. Foreman. The theatre stood at the corner of Theatre Street and Fishergate and was constructed at a cost of £3,000 ready for the start of the 1802 Guild celebrations. The building to the right is William Cartwright's house (now Littlewoods) (*Harris Ref. Lib.*)

great favour if they will please to comply with this request, and shall be exceedingly obliged to them for an early answer.

The committee agreed to his request and Cartwright built his house, the facade of which still stands and is incorporated into the new Littlewoods store on Fishergate.

### 27 October 1802 (*Gregson to J. Sturges & Co. and W. & J. Rigby*)

Gregson approached S. G. & J. Sturges & Company and W. & J. Rigby for a quotation to supply 100 Tons of iron rails.

### 28 October 1802 (*Jackson Mason to John Scale*)

The defective rails sent by the Aberdare Company were still languishing on the dockside at Liverpool and the company's solicitor wanted to know what Mr Scales intended to do about them:

> I am under the absolute necessity that the Cast Iron Rails you have sent they being extremely unfit for which purpose and quite contrary to your Contract – The rails are therefore laying at your risk, and you will give proper directions relating to them – it is unnecessary for me to add that you will not attempt to cast more iron rails for this Company.

## 9 November 1802 (*Gregson to Committee*)

In response to Mason's letter, John Scales journeyed to Liverpool and met Cartwright who had arranged for a random sample of the rails to be tested to destruction:

> The first rail weighed 39lb and broke with a weight equal to 3½ tons
> The second weighed 41lb and broke with a weight equal to 4¾ tons
> The third weighed 40lb and broke with a weight equal to 3¾ tons
> The fourth weighed 42lb and broke with a weight equal to 4 tons

Mr Scales could not dispute the inferior nature of his castings and was left with a problem. He now had a large tonnage of iron rusting away on the dockside which he would have to remove at his own expense or sell as scrap. Mr Cartwright kindly suggested a way of solving the problem by offering to buy the load at the cut price rate of £7 3s 4d. per ton. Mr Scales went off to consider the offer and after due consideration accepted it.

## 18 November 1802 (*Gregson to Sturges & Co.*)

Meanwhile Sturges & Company, of the Bowling Ironworks were preparing their tender for the supply of further iron rails and asked Gregson for clarification of the test which was to be employed in determining their quality:

> The rail is placed on two blocks at the same distances when laid – a lever is fixed on the middle of the rail and laden with weights until the rail breaks.

It was further pointed out that in previous tests, poor rails shattered when a 3½ ton force was applied whereas good quality rails could withstand a weight of 6 tons before they succumbed. It was therefore concluded that the specification required the rails to withstand a 5 ton force.

## 20 November 1802 (*Gregson to Sturges & Co.*)

When submitted, W. & J. Rigby & Company's tender was found to be too high and in any case they would not guarantee that their rails would carry the weight required in the specification. However J. Sturges and Company's tender was in the right area:

> We now have a Contract with a House in your part of the country who are delivering us a very good article at £10–5s per Ton laid down at Preston. If you can make any alterations in your offer I shall be glad to lay it before our Committee but it must be understood that we are to be supplied with your best strongest iron.

## 28 November 1802 (*Gregson to J. Sturges*)

Sturges & Company's tender was subsequently accepted and Gregson sent an order for 100 tons with the promise of more to come if found satisfactory. Mr Dickinson, the company's carpenter, was directed to carve another pattern rail ready for dispatch: 'The pattern rail will be sent off by Greenwood's if ready, if not it will be sent on by the same carrier.'

*The Construction of The Lancaster Canal Tramroad*

## 1 December 1802 (*Cartwright to Committee*)

The committee wanted to be kept informed of the progress of the tramroad, and Cartwright submitted a breakdown of the outstanding works together with cost estimates:

> The Rail Road is begun at Walton Summit and one Road is completed to near Kellet Lane, The Road is also begun at Preston, but the Contract which was made with Mr Scale not being fulfilled has greatly delayed the progress of the works. – Since the Contract was made with Aydon and Elwell we have obtained a regular supply of Iron Rails, which leaves me in no doubt that one Road will be completed by the 1 June 1803 which will greatly facilitate the Trade which the other is done which may be in the course of three months after that period.

### Transcript of Cartwright's Estimate of Cost for Finishing the Works Submitted to the Committee on 1st December 1802

| | yds | | £ | s | d |
|---|---|---|---|---|---|
| To forming banks over Ribble Valley etc etc | | | | | |
| To embanking in Mr. Dickinson's land from 2 chains north of lane | 400 | 6d | 100 | 0 | |
| To embanking in Mr. Watson's land | 3000 | 6d | 75 | 0 | 0 |
| To cutting on the inclined plane | 1000 | 6d | 25 | 0 | 0 |
| To making cop fencing and forming roads | 50 Roods | 8/2 | 20 | 8 | 4 |
| To dressing banks making approaches for roads, and laying plats | | | 50 | 0 | 0 |
| To ditto slopes in deep cutting to Preston Basin | | | 10 | 0 | 0 |
| To fencing with posts and rails | 1602 Roods | 6s | 480 | 12 | 0 |
| To setting quick fence 4½ miles double | | | 123 | 2 | 3 |
| To sundry gates and crop fences | | | 120 | 0 | 0 |
| To occupation roads footpaths etc | | | 50 | 0 | 0 |
| | | | £1147 | 2s | 7d |
| Iron Rails and laying the Road | Tons | | | | |
| To Rail Road 7957 yards long | 568 | £11 | 6248 | 0 | 0 |
| To splice roads and sundry wharfs 1400 yards long | 100 | £11 | 1100 | 0 | 0 |
| To additional strength rails for crossing roads say | | | 500 | 0 | 0 |
| To gad nails, plugs and sundry utensils | | | 300 | 0 | 0 |
| To waggons bringing materials on the road | 10 | £15 | 150 | 0 | 0 |
| To laying Rail Road | 1237 Roods | 70s | 4329 | 10 | 0 |
| To three inclined planes additional labour | | | 500 | 0 | 0 |
| To 3 small steam engines for the inclined planes | 3 | £350 | 1050 | 0 | 0 |
| To 3 engine houses, 3 frame rollers and gear | | | 450 | 0 | 0 |
| Materials provided and work done | | | 14627 | 10 | 0 |
| To iron rails purchased from Aydon & co. 7770 Rails | 1523-6-6 | | | | |
| To temporary Rail Roads now in use 61 Tons @ £11 | 671-0-0 | | | | |
| To Road laid 100 Roods | 150-0-0 | | | | |
| To stones prepared at Bamber Bridge 8000 Tons @ 5d | 166-13-4 | | | | |
| To ditto at Preston 2500 Tons @ 5d | 52-1-0 | | 2563 | 1 | 6 |
| | | | £12064 | 8s | 6d |
| Wharehouse and wharf walls at Preston | | | | | |
| To walling wharfs etc | | | 100 | 0 | 0 |
| To paving ditto | 9620 | 2s | 962 | 0 | 0 |
| To building warehouse (say) | | | 1000 | 0 | 0 |

| | | | | | |
|---|---|---|---|---|---|
| To making roads | 8448 | 1s | 422 | 8 | 0 |
| To Mr. Watson's fence wall | 348 | 6s | 104 | 8 | 0 |
| To stages and hurries over the Canal | | | 800 | 0 | 0 |
| | | | £3388 | 16s | 0d |
| Land | ARP | | | | |
| To Thomas Burscoughs | 3.3.3 | £100 | 378 | 17 | 16 |
| To land from Heatley to Brown Edge Lane | 2.2.0 | £150 | 375 | 0 | 0 |
| To Mr. Watsons land | 1.0.0 | | 300 | 0 | 0 |
| To Mr. Dickinsons ditto | 3.2.0 | | 525 | 0 | 0 |
| To Mr. Farringtons ditto | 1.3.0 | | 262 | 10 | 0 |
| To Mr. John Greens ditto | | | 150 | 0 | 0 |
| To Mr. Cross when the exchange with Canal Co. is made say | 2.0.0 | | 157 | 10 | 0 |
| To Mrs. Wharton's land | | | 800 | 0 | 0 |
| Temporary damages (say) | | | 500 | 0 | 0 |
| To Duke of Devonshire and Mr. Crook in Brindle | | | 1200 | 0 | 0 |
| To Mr. Heatley's | | | 402 | 15 | 0 |
| | | | £5051 | 12s | 6d |
| Bills unpaid | | | | | |
| To Mr. Ralph Ashton lot of ashwood | | | 67 | 0 | " |
| To Jeffrey Langshaw | | | 34 | 2 | 6 |
| To Summerfield and Atkinson | | | 1200 | 0 | " |
| To Ayden and Elwick | | | 1226 | 6 | 6 |
| To John Brockbank | | | 355 | 7 | 8 |
| To Halton Iron Co. | | | 130 | 7 | " |
| To R. Walton lot of timber | | | 8 | 17 | " |
| To James Norris | | | 0 | 12 | " |
| To Threlfall and Thistleton for timber | | | 208 | 18 | 9 |
| | | | 3231 | 11 | 5 |
| To one months pay due to the workmen | | | 1800 | 0 | 0 |
| | | | £5031 | 11s | 5d |

## 29 January 1803 (*Gregson to Cartwright*)

As for the defective rails from Aberdare, the Lancaster Company duly purchased the load, with the intention of using the best of them for whatever purpose they could be made use of. However, before Cartwright had chance to inspect them, an offer was made to purchase any which were of no use to the company:

> The committee having had application from Mr Park and from Sir Richard Clayton's Coal Company to supply them with part of the Iron Rails which came from Wales, and which are not of sufficient strength to place in the Rail Road from Walton Summit to Preston, they desire you will state to them what quantity of those rails there may remain to be disposed of after you have taken out such as will answer the purpose of the Canal Company.

## 2 February 1803 (*Cartwright to Gregson*)

The coal mine owners were destined to be disappointed when Cartwright found time to sort through the rails. He found that most of the rails were of sufficient strength to be incorporated within the less demanding areas of the tramroad:

I am getting the Rails which came from Wales sorted and taken away from Broomfield's Wharf, and I have the satisfaction to say that I don't think there will be more than 70 or 80 yards of waste rails more than what I can recommend to be used in the Limestone or ascending road passing places and splice roads. Rails of less strength than your Contract mentions I have no doubt will answer for the purposes I have mentioned.

The weather was affecting the works at that time:

The frost has stopped the laying of the Rail Road but I hope it will not delay the completion as there are many Carts employed getting materials to the Ground.

## 2 February 1803 (*Gregson to Aydon & Elwell*)

The weather was also affecting the delivery of the rails: 'Inclosed you will receive a Draft for £875 6s, the last parcel of rails are, I suppose, detained on the road by the frost.'

Plate Rail from the Walton Summit to Preston Tramroad.
This very rare and almost perfect specimen is on display at the South Ribble Museum and Exhibition Centre. (*S.B. – 1998*)

## 24 February 1803 (*Cartwright to Committee*)

Several ironworks were now engaged in casting rails of good quality and delivering them to site at a rate to satisfy the demands of the navvies: 'The Rail Road is going on rapidly, one road will be complete to Bamber Bridge in about 3 weeks.' The problems at Whittle Hills also seemed to be diminishing: '*The arching through the Tunnel through Whittle Hills will be completed in about eight weeks, and the Canal will be made navigable about that time.*'

The forming of the Walton Summit canal basin was to be left till later. The tramroad had priority:

> The cutting at Walton Summit will be our last job, and will not be done for some time, a Splice Road will be laid along the benching to bring gravel and stones for the Rail road. The Rail Road is begun in Ribble Valley, and I hope in the course of a few months we shall make great progress.

The company looked forward to a period of steady progress now that the problems of land purchase and rail supply had been resolved. However, it appears that each new phase of the works on the tramroad stirred up more trouble:

> We shall begin to put up the Steam Engine at Ribble next week for the first inclined plane. Mr Pilkington called at the office yesterday and told me that Sir H. Hoghton had received another opinion (Mr Woods) respecting the Canal Company erecting a Steam Engine for the purpose of working the inclined planes on each side of the Ribble Valley which was decisively against the Canal Company, in the same opinion he also says that the Canal Company had no right to lay the Rail Road, and advises Sir Henry to file a Bill in Chancery against them.

## 27 April 1803 (*Cartwright to Gregson*)

As the engine winding houses were taking shape at Avenham and Penwortham, Sir Henry Hoghton became agitated at the lack of consultation by the company. Like many others, he had been expecting a canal to pass through his lands, not a rail road and he certainly did not expect steam engines to be belching out smoke over his beloved Ribble valley. Cartwright was summoned to see Sir Henry's legal representative:

> I saw Mr Pilkington the Attorney yesterday who told me Sir Henry had given him directions to write to the Committee respecting the two small fire engines which are now erecting on each side the Ribble Valley.

Mr Pilkington intimated that Sir Henry was mainly aggrieved by the fact that nobody had had the courtesy of speaking with him and that a visit by some members of the committee might rectify any misunderstandings. Cartwright went on to suggest a way in which Sir Henry could be placated:

> If the gentlemen of the deputation write to Sir Henry, they may say that it is the Committee's intention to put up the Boilers of those small engines of the patent principal of burning the smoke by this very precaution it is hoped the engine will not be found to do the least injury.

## 15 May 1803 (*Gregson to Sir Henry Hoghton*)

Gregson apparently arranged to meet Sir Henry face to face to discuss the matter of the steam engines but for some reason the meeting did not take place and he therefore resorted to writing. He concluded that Sir Henry had got hold of the wrong end of the stick in thinking the engines were associated with drawing water up from the river rather than their actual and less demanding purpose in drawing waggons up a slope.

Having just received a letter from Mr Robert Hesketh suggesting the propriety of writing to you on the subject of our mission. I take the liberty of addressing you on the part of the Committee.

When the aforesaid Gentleman and myself went to Preston the other day, it was less for the purpose of making any proposals to you respecting the works in Ribble Valley, than to obviate some misunderstanding, that seemed to have arisen on the subject. For, not necessary to erect any Engine *for the purpose of raising water up to the Canal within the specified distance* but merely for the temporary purpose of serving a rail way, and subservient to the future execution of the original scheme, they conceived themselves sufficiently within the intent and meaning of the Act. They hoped moreover, that their intended engines being of small dimensions, 13in cylinders, or 6 Horse power, could not as things now stand, be considered even as a nuisance as, especially as they mean to consume the chief part of their smoke; when so many engines, incomparably larger, are smoking on every side, without any such means employed to diminish their effect.

They flattered themselves therefore, that a candid exposition of their views and objects would remove every difficulty from your mind. Had they been apprehensive, that what they propose could be considered contrary to the Act, or as serious nuisance to individuals, you must be sensible Sir, that there were and are means, by which they could have eluded the difficulty: but having no views, which they conceived objectionable, and meaning the rail way across the valley only as a temporary expedient of uniting the parts of their Canal, until the heavy expence of crossing on a level can be faced, they have proceeded to lay out a very serious sum of money to accomplish their object; and they must hope, that, on further consideration, you will see no objection sufficiently strong to induce you to oppose its completion.

If however after this statement, any such should remain they will be extremely happy, when acquainted with it, to give it every reasonable attention. Much more might undoubtedly be urged, and with better effect, had we had the advantage of a personal conference; but this much may suffice to show you the light, in which we have viewed the business.

In case Sir Henry had missed the point of the letter, Gregson added a post script:

you may conceive Sir, the difference between a 6 Horse engine, and one necessary for raising water out of the Ribble when you are informed that the latter is to be of 70 Horse power.

## 16 May 1803 (*Cartwright to the Committee*)

The committee required another report on progress.

The Rail Road from the Basins at Walton Summit to Preston is completed as follows.

First the Coal or descending Road from Walton Summit to Lea Brow Lane is down, being in length 666 Roods. The length from this place to the inclined plane at Mr Watson's Factory is 94 Roods which yet remains unfinished. – From this place to the junction with Dyson's work on the south side of Ribble Valley is 54 Roods making together 148 Roods which is the whole distance that is wanting to make the Coal or Descending Road complete. – The Limestone or Ascending Road is laid from Preston across the bridge into Ribble Valley and is now going on expeditiously.

# The Old Tram Road

One of the Steam Engines is put up at Avenham for working the Inclined Plane which is now complete within a few days work.

At the Inclined Plane at Mr Watson's Factory the Machinery is put up and the Steam Engine is made ready.

The unfinished parts are the Ascending Road being in length 950 Roods together with all the Fencing with Posts, Rails and Quicks.

The Wharfs want levelling and forming together with sundry jobs as stated in the General Account.

The progress of the Rail Road has been greatly retarded by bad weather being work which cannot be done in the Winter season without a great additional expence.

## 4 July 1803 (*Cartwright to the Committee*)

Two months later Cartwright submitted a final estimate of the outstanding works associated with the tramroad.

> The works are prosecuting as fast as circumstances will allow. – The Coal or descending Rail Road from the Basin at Walton Summit to Preston is laid, excepting the inclined plane on the south side the Ribble Valley, which is now in execution and will be finished in about nine days.
>
> The Limestone or ascending Rail Road is laid from the Basin at Preston into the Ribble Valley, and is now proceeding with, and going on in several places, and I hope will be complete in November next.

## 5 July 1803 (*Committee Meeting*)

As the tramroad neared completion, the company turned its attentions to setting up a scale of charges:

> Upon all Coal, Cannel Coal and Cinders which shall be navigated or carried between Walton Summit aforesaid and the Town of Preston a Tonnage Duty shall be paid of two shillings and three pence per Ton (of the like weight)
>
> Upon all Coal, Cannel Coal and Cinders which shall be navigated or carried between Walton Summit aforesaid and the inclined plane on the south side of the Ribble a Tonnage Duty shall be paid of One shilling and nine pence per Ton (of the like weight)
>
> Upon all Coal, Cannel Coal and Cinders

Notice of Intention to Let wharfage at the Preston and Walton Summit Basins. The notice, which appeared in the Lancaster Gazette, was perhaps a little premature for it would be a further twelve months before the basins would be open for business. (*Harris Ref. Lib.*)

> "On the first instant, a boat laden with coal was navigated on the Lancaster Canal thro' the tunnel at Whittle Hills, and her cargo was discharged into waggons at the termination of the canal at Walton. Twenty seven waggons were laden, each containing about one ton, and were drawn by one horse, a mile and a half, along the rail road, to the works of Messrs Claytons at Bamber Bridge. The waggons extended one hundred yards in length along the rail road, Geo. Clayton of Lostock Hall Esq., rode upon the first waggon and the tops of the others were fully occupied. The intention of navigating a boat through the Tunnel, upon this day, was not generally known; it was quickly circulated; old and young left their habitations and emoluments to witness a sight so novel, and before the boat reached her discharging place, she was completely crowded with passengers, who anxiously rushed into her at every bridge. The workmen were regaled with ail, at Bamber Bridge; and among the toasts of the party were given, 'the glorious First of June', 'the Memory of Lord Howe', and 'The health of the surviving heroes of that memorable day'.
>
> *Blackburn Mail – June 1803*

which shall be navigated or carried between Walton Summit aforesaid and a certain Road or Lane called Toad Lane in the Township of Walton le Dale a Tonnage Duty shall be paid of one shilling and two pence per Ton (of the like weight)

Upon all Coal, Cannel Coal and Cinders which shall be navigated or carried between Walton Summit aforesaid and the Turnpike Road at or near Bamber Bridge in the said Township of Walton le dale a Tonnage Duty shall be paid of seven pence per Ton (of the like weight)

## 15 July 1803 (*Gregson to Cartwright*)

As the steam engine at Avenham was commissioned, early trials seemed to indicate that it may not be powerful enough to haul the waggons, and news of these doubts reached Gregson:

> We have had a Committee meeting this morning and Dr Rigby mentioned that it was accurately reported in Preston that the steam engine at the inclined planes at Ribble were not of sufficient power to perform the work required of them, it was also said that upon trial, the engine would scarcely turn the chain – The Committee have desired me to write to you and request that you will state how this matter stands and if there has been any error in the calculations or construction at the inclined plane, whether you are taking proper measures to remedy the evil – I shall thank you for an answer by return of post.

## 17 July 1803 (*Cartwright to Gregson*)

No doubt Cartwright was stung by the tone of Gregson's letter questioning his professional judgement and he lost no time in firing off a reply:

> I received your favour, in reply there can be no doubt but the steam engines at Avenham will have sufficient power, Its true the chain takes more power to work it than expected and had the engines been made to the calculations Messrs Jessop and Rennie left with me I believe would have been insufficient – The calculation states that 3½ horses power would be sufficient

*The Old Tram Road*

> 2. Compleating the Iron Rail Road.
> Inclined plane at Walton Summit  57R 6/  129 11 „
> Forming do. & taking out Slips . . . . . . . . . . . 150 „ .
> Laying of the Roads at Walton Summit B  65R 3/6  102 7 6
> Finishing do. which is begun . . . .  36 „  56 14 „
> Laying one Road at Walton Summit to the Inclined plane at Mr. Watsons Tract  977 3/  1465 10 „
> Finishing single Road . . . .  577 „  865 „ . .
> Inclined plane at Mr. Watsons  21 70  73 10 . .
> Lying & compleating Rail Road across Ribble Valley . . . .  170 16/  136 „ . .
> do. finishing Dysons work do  63 „  50. 8 .
> Inclined plane at Avenham  60 6/  180 „ . „
> Posts & Rails Lucks, Inverts, Gates &c  2263 9/  1018 11 „
> Engine House at Mr. Watsons . . . .  100 „ .
> Chain for Inclined plane . . . .  300 „ „
> Fixing up the Frame at Walton Summit & Rollers for both planes . . . .  100 „ „
> Filling the Rail Road to top of the Flanches  555 3/6  271. 19 „
> Iron Rails wanting . . .  70 Tons . . .  840 „ . .
> Waggons & utinsels . . . .  500
> £ 6339. 10. 6

Page From the Lancaster Canal Co. Letter Book 4th July 1803.
William Cartwright's estimate of cost for completing the Tramroad. (P.R.O.)

– The engines in question are made equal to 6 horses power which leave no doubt with me but they will answer the purpose intended.

The report stated in your letter arose from the workman who was fixing up the engine, trying to set the machine in question to work before the shafts and other things were made complete, exactly the same manner as the weighing machine at Lancaster (you may recollect it was reported all over Town that it would not answer the purpose).

He went on to snipe at local employers for affecting the progress of the works:

The Engineers and Mill Wrights in the Town have done little or nothing this last 3 weeks on account of lowering their wages, otherwise the inclined plane would have been completed before this, and the waggons passing materials for the works in the valley.

## 25 July 1803 (*Gregson to Edward Tatham*)

Away from the steam engines, the rest of the works were progressing well until the navvies began to run out of stone sleepers. The nearest quarry was closed and Cartwright, determined not to see his works suffer, sent his own men in to cut, dress and bore as many sleepers as were needed to keep the navvies supplied. Some time later Gregson received a bill from the quarry owner:

> About a month ago Mr Cartwright settled with Burton, one of the partners in the Whittle Hill Quarry, for all the stones which had been got. Since that time we wanted a parcel of Rail way stones getting but the quarry men were busy with their cottage houses that they could not get them within the time they were wanted: as the work could not be detained the men were ordered to get for themselves.
>
> The Canal Company have been at great expence in opening the quarry in Whittle Hills, for which the renters have not made any allowance and if they would have got stone Mr Cartwright would not have directed the workmen to begin for themselves. I do not imagine that it is any quantity of stone that is required – and we shall be willing to make reasonable allowance to the renters of the quarry

## 29 August 1803 (*Gregson to John Scales*)

Despite the Aberdare Iron Company's failure at the beginning of the contract. Gregson now accepted an offer to supply a small quantity of rails at a price much lower than that agreed almost eighteen months previous:

> The Lancaster Canal Company will accept the offer contained in the said letter, say for about 40 Tons of rail plates delivered at Preston at 9 guineas per Ton.

## 29 September 1803 (*Gregson to Committee*)

Any worries about the capabilities of the steam engines seem to have evaporated when Gregson reported to the committee on progress of the inclined planes at the Ribble:

> The steam engine and inclined plane on the south side of Ribble Valley is nearly ready. On the north side the whole is complete.

## 3 October 1803 (*Cartwright to Gregson*)

The day when the two ends of the canal were to be united was now in sight and, with mounting enthusiasm, Cartwright gave Gregson a brief report of the remaining works:

> The Canal and Rail Road from Johnson's Hillock to Preston are in great forwardness, and as soon as there is water to fill the Canal the Trade may be opened to Preston.
>
> The setting up of the engine near Mr Watson's will be completed in about nine days. – The laying of the double road will be done in about a month, – The inclined plane and splice roads at Walton Summit are intended not to begin until the whole of the other road is finished.

*The Old Tram Road*

## 20 November 1803 (*Cartwright to Gregson*)

At last the canal was completed through to Walton Summit and all was ready to let the water in. It was fairly normal for sections of a canal to leak when water was introduced for the first time and this was true of the section to Walton Summit. The cut had to be emptied of water to allow the navvies to work the clay puddle and seal the leak. Cartwright informed Gregson of his proposals and at the same time reported on the completion of the Coal Road:

> The water will be let into this part of the Canal again on Saturday and I expect about the middle of next week, coals may be brought to Walton Summit and along the Rail Road to Preston.

Cartwright needed to know how the wharves were to be split up at the summit basin:

> The Committee will therefore please to send me directions how I am to divide the Wharfs at Walton Summit. I am laying a main Rail Road parallel with the east arm of the Basin and putting out splice roads at every boats length in an oblique direction to hold 4 waggons,

*P*LAN *of the Basin and* Inclined Plane *on the*
*L*ANCASTER *C*ANAL *at the end of the Summit Level.*

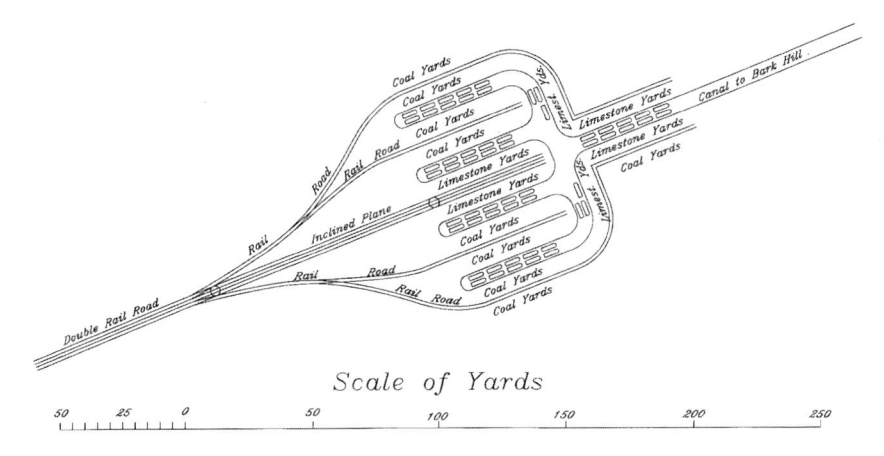

*William Cartwright 1801*

Walton Summit Basin.
This is what the Basin was intended to look like. In fact the outer arms were never constructed due to lack of finances. The inclined plane was soon abandoned when it was found that the horses could work the tracks on either side which were of a lesser gradient.
(Based on drawing in *P.R.O.*)

52

The tramroad could not operate until a scale of charges had been prepared and Cartwright put forward his own views:

> for the Wharfage and use of the Waggons, one penny per Ton in addition to the Canal Duty should be charged. For the use of the Canal Company's Railway Waggons I think 4d per Ton should be taken for Coal and 2d for Limestone. Little experience will point out their value together with their wear, tear, and oiling the wheels, the price may then be varied by the Committee when the real value is known.

The works at the Preston Basin were nearly complete:

> The Stages and Hurrys at Preston are making for three boats to load, one of which will be finished next week.

This turned out to be William Cartwright's final letter to Samuel Gregson. As the canal on which he had toiled for so many years stood on the threshold of achieving its main purpose, he was taken ill and within two months was dead.

## 25 November 1803 (*Gregson to Cartwright*)

Gregson, unaware of Cartwright's approaching illness, replied to his request for instructions upon how to lay out the wharves at the Summit. The coal mine owners were to have preference and the Earl of Balcarras, Sir Richard Clayton, Mr Johnson and Mr Hollinshead were to be allocated two boat lengths each. Gregson went further and outlined the way in which the loading and unloading of the barges and waggons was to be effected:

> and it is the directions of the company that until such time as the Rail way is complete the different yards allotted out to any Trader who has a boat to discharge and waggons ready to receive the coal, shall be admitted to unload his boat at any railed road where there is a vacancy, and no person (altho' the yard may be allocated to him) shall prevent such boat from discharging when the Rail road is unemployed.

Gregson agreed with Cartwright's suggested charges for using the tramroad and went on to discuss the supply of waggons:

> I apprehend there will some difficulty arise in arranging the number of waggons to be let to each Trader in the first instance – it strikes me at present that as the Boats come up they must be supplied with so many waggons as will carry their load to Preston in one day, that is if a Boat should bring about 30 Tons the Trader should be supplied with 8 waggons which he should be obliged to make two trips in a day would remove 32 Tons – of course 24 waggons would suffice 3 Traders and would bring 96 Tons per day – as the water is at present, 4 waggons will discharge a Boat in a day. These matters may be improved upon after they are tried.

At Preston, the traders would have to make the best of it until the basin was finished off:

> The want of conveniences at Preston for laying down Coal, and of a Weighing Machine will

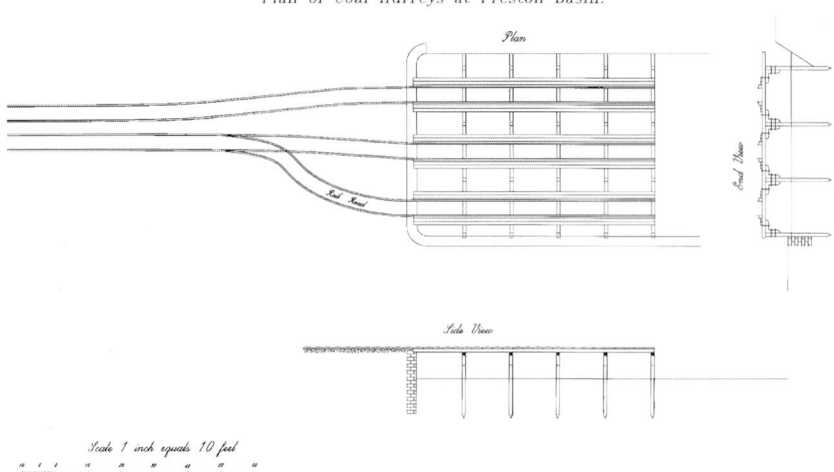

Plan of Coal Hurreys at Preston Basin.

Timber coal hurreys at Preston Basin.
The 'Hurreys' were built over the end of the canal to enable fully laden waggons to run over the top in order to discharge their cargoes directly into the barges waiting below.
(Based on drawing in *P.R.O.*)

make inconvenience for the Traders at first, and I think their best plan will be to ship all they bring by waggons on this part of the Canal.

## 12 January 1804 (*Gregson to Mr Pilkington*)

The arguments about the steam engines at the Ribble valley rumbled on. In order to gain acceptance of the steam engines at Avenham and Penwortham from Sir Henry Hoghton the company had to enter into a bond which, amongst other restrictions, specified the maximum size of engine to be set to work on the inclined planes.

The company decided to hold off from signing the bond until the engines were up and running in the hope that upon seeing them working and observing only minimal disruption, Sir Henry might drop his objections.

> The Bond to Sir H. P. Hoghton and Mr Starkie has most certainly been delayed by the Committee and I trust that the reason for the delay (which I shall give you) will prove satisfactory. It must be evident to you that the point in question, is of very serious moment to the Canal Company, and it was the desire of the Company to try the effect of the Steam Engines already erected, not only to give the Gentlemen interested an idea how far they might prove the nuisance these were supposed to be but also to try their effect in performing the work they were intended to do. From the trials which have hitherto been made, the Committee have great confidence the Gentlemen will perceive that the nuisance arising from them is not by any means equal to what they first apprehended, and they hope that the addition of a few inches to the Diameter of the Cylinder will not become an objection on the part of Sir

H. Hoghton or Mr Starkie, if it should be found necessary to increase their power at any future period.

The business of the payment for the stone sleepers was again raised:

> The remaining fact of your letter I cannot answer explicitly as I would wish until I hear from Mr Cartwright: of this you may be assured that the committee are ready to make every reasonable recompense to the lessees of Whittle Hill Quarry, incase the same has not been already done,

Cartwright would be unable to help Gregson as he was now confined to his bed with a rapidly worsening condition.

In addition to the question of payment for the sleepers, Sir Henry's solicitor went on to accuse the canal company of allowing their men to sell off stone from the quarry and pocketing the proceeds. Gregson countered:

> With respect to the sale of rubble or other stone to the public by the workmen I will venture to assert (altho' I know nothing of the circumstances) that whatever has been done in that way, has been done without any order or authority from the Canal Company or their agents, and I am certain the Company have not reaped any benefit whatsoever there from. I apprehend that the individuals who carried on the transaction are answerable to the lessees of the Quarry for their conduct.

Looking to the future, the company thought that the size of the engines allowed for in the bond may prove critical to the development of the tramroad and Gregson strove to have the size of the cylinders increased:

> Since writing the above I have seen some of the Gentlemen of our Committee, who are of opinion that 20 inch Cylinders will be equal to any power that may be wanted for the Trade, and if Sir H. Hoghton and Mr Starkie would extend the power from 16 to 20 inches in the present Bond the same would be immediately executed and returned without any other alteration.

## 6 February 1804 (*Gregson to James Fergus*)

William Cartwright died on 19 January leaving Gregson to take on many of his duties in addition to his own. His first priority was to finish the installation of the weighing machine at Walton Summit:

> The Iron for the top of the Machine will be drawn at the Forge – it will be a few days before it is ready. I have ordered some steel to be sent which should have come by the Boat this day if the Frost had not continued.

## 10 February 1804 (*Gregson to Fergus*)

Until a replacement engineer could be appointed Gregson was forced to deal directly with the contractor, and issued instructions pertaining to the construction of the Preston basin:

> The carrying on the works at the foot of the slope thro' the cutting near Fishergate should be attended to, you will have a parcel of stone sleepers sent for the purpose. I think the walls

# The Old Tram Road

around the outside of the Basins and Yards should be of the following dimensions – Height 6 feet and a coping – breadth at bottom 22 inches – breadth at top 14 inches. To be walled in mortar and stone scabelled and coursed.

The wheels for the waggons were ordered to be cast, which when completed, would signal the end a number of tradesmen's association with the canal:

> I have ordered wheels to be cast for 20 waggons, and it is the opinion of the committee that as soon as those are complete there should be no more Carpenters and Smiths kept than what will be necessary for the works, I suppose Robert Easterby and two other Smiths will be sufficient.

## 11 February 1804 (*Gregson to D. Lewis*)

As the various buildings and wharves were completed at Preston the tenants made ready to move in:

> The Committee will let you the warehouse for a term of 31 years at the yearly rent of Twenty Guineas including the privilege of taking condensing water from the Canal.

## 15 February 1804 (*Gregson to John Watson*)

The company had still not signed the bond for the steam engines with Sir Henry Hoghton. Gregson sought to break the deadlock by approaching Mr Watson with whom he was now on good terms:

> I laid your letter of the 10th inst. before a meeting of the Canal Committee held yesterday, They are anxious to have Sir H. P. Hoghtons, and Mr Starkies consent to enlarge the Steam Engines at Ribble to 18 inches Cylinder – and from your letter they apprehend there may not be much difficulty in obtaining it. – The Bonds between the Canal Company and those Gentlemen are not yet executed and the Committee wish me to suggest that through your application to Mr Pilkington the Gentlemen might give liberty to insert 18 inches in the Bond – I wrote to Mr Pilkington some time ago and proposed 20 inches Cylinder, this Sir Henry rejected, but if a consent to 18 inches could be obtained there can be no doubts of it answering every purpose which the public may expect from the work.

Mr Watson had previously complained about the steam engine adjacent to his land, and more specifically the small reservoirs associated with it, being sited at the top of the incline at Penwortham. Gregson agreed to move it:

> When the Engine is removed to the bottom of the hill your apprehensions with respect to water will be done away – at present the Committee trust you will not do any thing to injure or interrupt he works.

## 16 February 1804 (*Gregson to Fergus*)

The installation of the weighing machines now occupied Gregsons attention:

> The iron for the top plates of the Weighing Machines is mainly all on board the Packet Boat and will come as soon as the weather will permit – The top of the machine pit walls are covered here with 4 large stones and there is a plate of iron fixed round the stones to guard

from slips and approach mainly to the top frames – you will find 4 Bars of iron for the purpose for each Machine – you may be going with the one at Brindle Wharf as soon as you have the frame ready.

## 17 February 1804 (*Gregson to Fergus*)

Work on the Preston basin was drawing to a close and Gregson was anxious for its completion without further incident:

> I think the coping on the south side the Basin should be put on before the Boats begin to discharge the stones for the walls if it is not they will be throwing the present course off their beds – you had best send the smoothing iron for coping stones.

## 17 April 1804 (*Gregson to Fergus*)

Until the weighing machines were fully installed, the waggons were not allowed to run on the tramroad. Without the ability to measure the loads, the correct tolls could not be charged and more importantly any extra heavy loads could shatter the rails. The installation of the weighing machines therefore rose to prominence as the number one job to be completed:

> You must get forward with the Weighing Machine on the Rail Road near Bamber Bridge as far as possible and the next Machine will be wanted on the Rail Road near Avenham for the Limestone Trade etc.

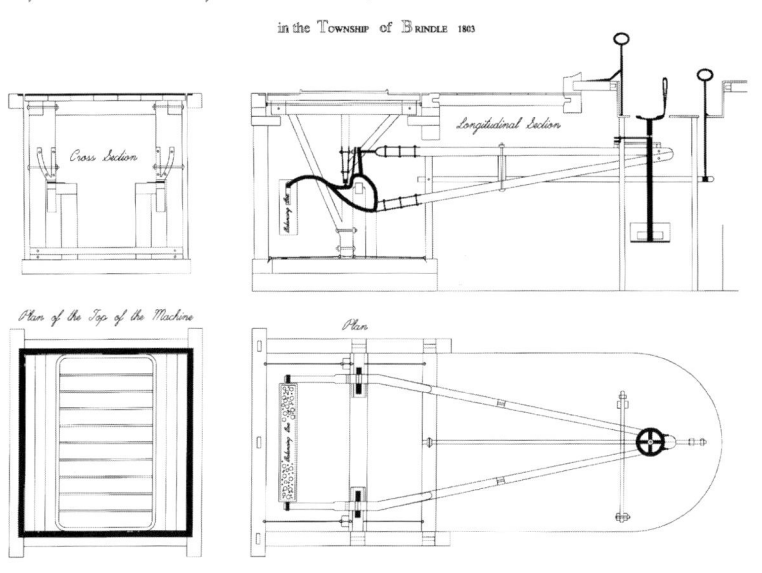

Weighbridge Mechanism at Walton Summit.
All waggons had to be weighed in order to levy the correct tolls and also to protect the rails from excessive loads. (Based on drawing in *P.R.O.*)

Model of a Tramroad Waggon on display in the Harris Museum, Preston.
(S.B. – 1998)

Cast iron wheel from a Lancaster Canal Tramroad Waggon.
Possibly the only remaining example. Recovered by divers from the bed of the River Ribble beneath the Old Tram Bridge. Currently on display in the Harris Museum.
(S.B. – 1998)

Gregson foresaw a problem with the waggons presently being built by Summerfield & Atkinson. The winding engines were to haul the waggons up the incline by means of an endless chain, running on rollers positioned between the ascending and descending roads, to which the waggons would be attached by means of iron staves mounted on the body. The staves provided with the waggons were not thought suitable and Gregson ordered the company smith's to forge new ones of increased strength. They were to be fixed to each corner of the waggon as close to the corners as practicable:

There are 14 Waggons at Summerfield's which must be delivered to the Canal Company. – It will be very well for Easterby to get a sufficient number of Iron staves to fix upon them – and I am inclined to think that if those staves are fixed nearer to the ends of the waggons they will have a better effect upon the inclined planes – I apprehend Mr Haliburton and others will be applying for Waggons, and I should have those made ready as fast as possible – The present axles must be tried, and the Smiths keep putting in the strongest arms by degrees as the waggons can be spared – you must pay particular attention that the Waggons which come from Summerfield's are in proper *gauge*, and in every respect complete except the staves which we are to renew.

The waggons were originally designed to carry a load of 2 tons and bore a strong resemblance to the agricultural carts in common use at the time. The wheelbase of the waggons was set so as to minimise the stress imposed on the rails by ensuring that the front wheel had passed onto the next rail before the rear wheels acted on the first. This ensured that each rail would be subjected to no more than one quarter of the total weight of waggon and cargo.

## 7 July 1804 (*Lancaster Gazette*)

With both roads of the tramroad now open for business, the proprietors looked forward to good times ahead and an announcement appeared in the Lancaster Gazette:

The completion of the tramroad heralded an upturn in the fortunes of the canal. Gross income for the year before the tramroad was opened was recorded as £4,583 but in 1804, although the tramroad was still incomplete for the early part, the income shot up to £8,490.

The turnpike at Bamber Bridge saw an immediate advantage in the completed tramroad:

> We understand, the General Meeting of the Lancaster Canal Proprietors, on Tuesday last, was most fully attended, and by many very respectable Proprietors from a distance. The business which came before the meeting, gave great satisfaction; and we sincerely hope, that the difficulties attending the arduous and important undertaking are now overcame. The least we can say is, to join our thanks with those of the public, for the very great reduction in the price of coal, which has taken place since the communication to the south part of the canal has been effected.

---

### LIME STONE WANTED

FOR REPAIRING the TURNPIKE ROADS, several THOUSAND TONS of LIME STONE, to be delivered by stated monthly quantities, at the place where the Rail-road crosses the turnpike road, near Bamber Bridge.

Any person desirous to contract for supplying same is requested to send proposals to Mr. Winstanley, of Preston, immediately; and to say, at what price he will deliver it, in the three following states, viz. as it arises from the delf; broken in pieces sufficiently small to be put upon the roads; and what is generally called lime stone gravel.

*Preston, Dec., 1804.*

# William Cartwright

Towards the end of 1793, William Cartwright was looking for a job. For several years he had been engaged in cutting the Basingstoke Canal but as the undertaking was nearing completion it was now time to move on.

At this time "Canal Mania" was at its zenith and good engineers were hard to find. In January 1794 The Lancaster Canal Company, desperate for expertise snapped up Cartwright for an annual salary of £400. Initially, he was employed to supervise the construction of the foundations for the Lune Aqueduct but as this crucial work ended he was elevated to Resident Engineer for the whole of the canal.

If any one man was responsible for the creation of the Walton Summit to Preston Basin Tramroad, that man was William Cartwright.

John Rennie and William Jessop were the chief engineers but, such was their stature, they were in demand throughout the country and were, as a consequence, engaged on several major projects simultaneously, leaving only minimal time for their Lancaster undertaking. It was left to Cartwright to ensure that the Tramroad was constructed in a proper manner, within the company's budgetary constraints and in the shortest time possible. He must have been in good spirits as 1803 drew to a close, with the Tramroad nearing completion and the Whittle Hills having been successfully tunnelled

William Cartwright's House.
When the Littlewoods building was erected, one of the briefs to the Architect was to retain and incorporate the frontage of the existing building into the new. The ground floor is modern but the elegant freestone facade above is that of William Cartwright's mansion which he had constructed in 1802. (S.B. – 1998)

through. At last the canal on which he had toiled for ten long years would start earning some real money, allowing the company to pay off some of its debts and to progress the cut northwards towards Kendal.

Tragically, William Cartwright was never to witness the fruits of his labours. He died, following a short illness, on 19th January 1804. His departure appears to have been fairly rapid and unexpected for he left no will and his wife Jane was forced to apply to the courts for the estate which was valued at £10,000. Like many of his contemporaries, his life-span was probably foreshortened as a result of overwork and the stress brought on by dealing with a demanding client and uncooperative contractors and perhaps by the regular exposure to too many northern winters.

> Mr. Wm Cartwright, whose death was announced last week was only in his 39th year, though his appearance was that of a much older man. His abilities and his judgement were equally mature.
>
> He possessed a happy cheeriness of temper, which gained him the esteem of all who had the pleasure of knowing him, and which made the workmen, employed under him, execute his commands with a promptitude which few could excite. In the year 1794, he came to Lancaster as resident engineer to the Lancaster Canal Company. His rapid execution of the piers on the Lune Aqueduct, was the astonishment of everyone, and must long remain in the remembrance of those, who were witness to his exertion and indefatigable attention in that most arduous work; the whole of which, although it rests on very unequal strata, remains without a crack, or the least variation. For some years, he has been the principal engineer to the Lancaster Canal Company; and the works which have been executed under his direction, will remain lasting and honourable monuments to his memory. What seldom falls to the lot of one man, was united in him − −a strong theoretical genius, accompanied by practical knowledge in every branch, and a persevering spirit, that overcame all difficulties. The loss of such a man, at so early an age, will be seriously felt in the public concerns which he was engaged.
>
> *Lancaster Gazette 21st January 1804*

Like many of his contemporaries William Cartwright was engaged on a variety of civil engineering projects during his lifetime. Among his more notable achievements was the design and installation of the Croston Drainage Scheme at the River Douglas which cost £6000 to complete.

He also worked with his brother Thomas, who was a respected engineer in his own right, on a survey to install tramroads in South Wales.

At the time of his death he was engaged in preparing a scheme for providing a tramroad between Tewitfield and the Kellet Seed Quarries and in constructing a tunnel between the River Ribble and Preston to enable water to be pumped to the canal.

## The Main Features of the Tramroad

The Walton Summit to Preston Basin Tramroad contained seven elements which were found necessary to effect a communion with the canal and to overcome natures obstacles. A waggon travelling along the Coal Road would be loaded at the Walton Summit Basin, then lowered down the inclined planes at the Summit and at Penwortham before traversing the Ribble via the timber bridge whereupon it would be hauled out of the valley up the Avenham inclined plane. There followed an easy run under Fishergate through the tunnel to discharge the coal into a waiting barge at the Preston Basin.

### Walton Summit Basin

In 1801, William Cartwright prepared a plan for the Walton Summit Basin which took the form of four arms extending beyond the end of the canal and parallel to its line. Each arm was to be 150yds long and able to accommodate ten barges, two abreast. In July the outline of the basin was set out on site and Cartwright asked Gregson to arrange for the purchase of the necessary land. Fields owned by The Duke of Devonshire, Thomas Burscough and Miss Headley were duly acquired.

The navvies got on with their task and as the summer of 1802 approached the finishing touches were being applied.

Only the inner two of the arms were constructed, which were later increased in length by 30 yards to allow their ends to turn inwards. In addition, a 30yd length was formed down the centre which was to terminate in a transhipment shed which covered the central wharves.

Sufficient land was purchased in order to accommodate the additional arms at some

Walton Summit Basin looking north.
This photograph taken in 1953 shows the two outer arms of the basin together with the central leg which allowed barges to manoeuvre inside the transhipment shed. The centre wall of the shed can be seen. (*G.Biddle*)

## The Main Features of the Tramroad

future date. However, trade never increased sufficiently to warrant their construction before the railways began to take business away from the canal.

A track laid from the Limestone Road served the wharves on the outside of the eastern arm and a system of sidings emanating from the coal road served all the others.

A plan of the basin prepared in 1803 shows the various wharves occupied by The Earl of Balcarras, Mr McKenzie and Company, Lawrence Bradshaw, Hale & Company, and Mr J. Hodgson.

It was necessary to check the weight of materials carried by the waggons on the tramroad in order to charge the correct tolls and to protect the plates from overloading.

Walton Summit Basin – 1952.
Close up of the central wall of the transhipment shed. (*G.Biddle*)

Walton Summit Basin – 1968.
Possible track bed of the Tramroad running adjacent to the canal basin. (*G.Biddle*)

*The Old Tram Road*

The Walton Summit Weighbridge House, Gough Lane.
This photograph taken in 1959 shows the weighbridge house in good condition, sporting freshly pointed stonework. Unfortunately the building was subsequently demolished. (*G.Biddle*)

To this end, a weigh bridge was installed about 500 yards north of the basin. For some reason the weighing machine was subsequently moved even further north to a point close to Gough Lane. The stone built machine house which contained the balancing mechanism survived until recently.

The Walton Summit Basin carried out its business, with little further change, for the life of the tramroad whereupon it was abandoned to gradually decay until all traces of it were eradicated when it was filled in during 1968.

## Walton Summit Incline

The Walton Summit Inclined Plane was the last to be completed and the first to be taken out of service.

William Cartwright's initial plan was to site a steam powered winding engine at the top of the incline to haul the limestone waggons up a 1 in 10 × 274yd long slope. The waggons loaded with coal were to take a separate track following the natural fall of the land. In fact, a plane with the somewhat easier gradient of 1 in 13 was installed.

The main line of the tramroad ascended the inclined plane and ran into the central area of the canal basin. Near the foot of the incline a siding, referred to as a spurring, split off the Limestone Road towards the eastern arm of the basin and likewise a spurring from the Coal Road served the western arm. The spurrings were of an easier gradient than the main line and could be worked by horses.

Some time before 1813 it was decided to abandon the inclined plane and modify the western spurring to provide access to the central area of the basin.

## The Main Features of the Tramroad

Walton Summit Incline – 1953.
The track bed of the inclined plane can be seen to the left of the photograph.
The stone sleepers have been reused to form a farm access road which occupies the centre
of the picture. (*G.Biddle*)

It seems strange that the Walton Summit inclined plane ever came into existence. Even as it was being constructed, Cartwright borrowed the steam winding engine to use as a temporary water pump at Preston in the knowledge that only minimum disruption would be experienced as the waggons were hauled along the spurrings by horse power.

On reflection, I think it possible that the inclined plane may have never been put into service. Once the trade was seen to operate efficiently using the spurrings it may have seemed pointless to incur further expense in completing an inclined plane that was in effect unnecessary. At present this theory, is pure speculation on my part and requires further investigation.

### *Penwortham Incline*

In order to haul the waggons out of the southern side of the Ribble valley, an engine worked inclined plane identical to that at Avenham was proposed. The Penwortham Incline Plane was to be sited near Carr Wood on land owned by Mr Watson who also owned the Penwortham Factory standing at the end of Factory Lane, now known as Vernon's.

William Cartwright envisaged a 1 in 9 slope × 232yds long, rising some 74ft and being worked by a steam powered winding engine situated at the top of the gradient.

When Messrs. Jessop and Rennie were asked to review Cartwright's plan they recommended that the gradient be made shorter and steeper and it was this revised

*The Old Tram Road*

form which was constructed. The gradient was exceedingly steep at 1 in 4.5 and 61ft 4ins in height. The engine house, together with its two small reservoirs, was sited at the top of the incline on the eastern side of the tramroad on land now enclosed by Carr Wood Farm. Mr Watson objected to the siting of the winding house and the company subsequently agreed to reposition it at the foot of the slope. However it seems that this proposed alteration was never acted upon.

The Penwortham inclined plane duly came into service in 1803, and no doubt was beset by similar problems in operation as its counterpart across the river. The company experimented with a newly patented twist link chain. Within eighteen months it had stretched by one tenth of its length and within the year had broken, no doubt with tragic consequences.

The inclined planes were perceived as unwelcome interruptions to the otherwise smooth operation of the tramroad and the committee engaged a number of engineers over the years to look into ways of eliminating them. The Avenham Incline could not be avoided, but in 1818 a viable alternative to the Penwortham Inclined Plane was developed.

A detailed survey showed that the land to the west of the inclined plane offered the potential for a longer and consequently easier gradient. The company, desperate to rid itself of the inconvenience, bought parts of the fields known as Haslem Field, Bronny Field and Ryding Meadow in order to accommodate the revised route. The new road bed took the form of a sweeping ark some 370yds in length and rising at a rate of 1 in 18.5 which was deemed suitable to be worked by horses.

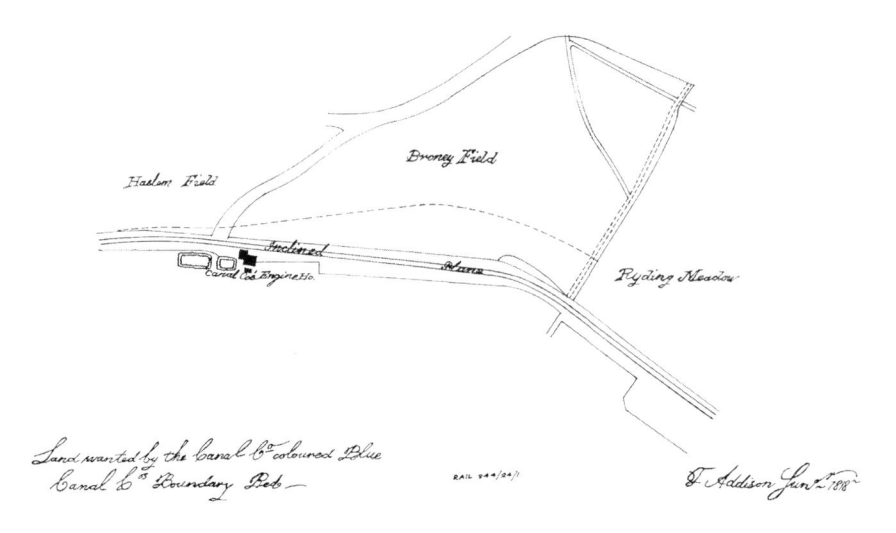

Modifications to the Penwortham Incline.
This drawing was prepared in 1818 by Thomas Addison Junior in order to purchase sufficient land to enable the company to abandon the Penwortham Inclined Plane. The red boundary referred to is to the western side of the track, and the area referred to as coloured blue lay between the red boundary and the broken line. The original road bed of the Inclined Plane can still be seen today. (P.R.O.)

## The Main Features of the Tramroad

Penwortham Incline – 1953.
This photograph looks northwards towards the top of the Penwortham Incline. Several stone sleepers can be seen still in situ. (*G.Biddle*)

By 1820 the diversion was complete and the Penwortham Inclined Plane, after working for only seventeen years, was taken out of service. The plates were lifted, no doubt to be used elsewhere, and the winding house was demolished. Probably the valuable steam engine was sold and put to another use.

Surprisingly, even after all these years, the original road bed for the Penwortham Inclined Plane can still be seen if one looks over the fence down onto Carr Hill Residential Park as the Old Tram Road begins its ascent out of the Ribble valley.

## *Avenham Incline*

Of the three inclines, the Avenham incline is the best documented and was the only one to remain in operation throughout the life of the tramroad.

Cartwright's original plan, prepared in 1801, shows an inclined plane rising 51ft at a gradient of 1 in 9 worked by a steam powered winding engine positioned at the top of the slope. The gradient was altered, presumably by Rennie and Jessop, to 1 in 6. They went on to recommend an engine of 3½ horsepower to haul the waggons.

Early in 1803, as the navvies toiled to prepare the road bed of the inclined plane ready to receive the dual track. The stonemasons, working in brick for a change, commenced the erection of the engine house. It was normal practice, at that time, for steam engines to be installed as an integral part of the engine house, with the very fabric of the building supporting and restraining the iron beast. Cartwright ignored

*The Old Tram Road*

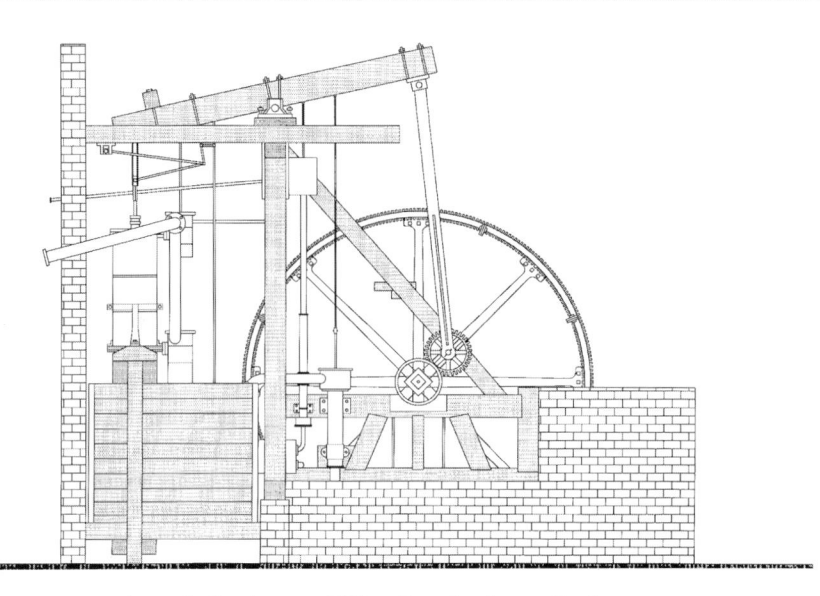

An early Boulton and Watt Rotative Steam Engine.
A similar type of machine would have been built into the Avenham Engine House.

The Avenham Engine House.
This photograph was taken shortly before the engine house was demolished in 1869 and shows part of the inclined plane and winding gear.
(*Harris Museum*)

Rennie and Jessop's recommendations and ordered three small engines of 6 horsepower with 13ins cylinders to work the inclines. Summerfield and Atkinson supplied the engines which Cartwright estimated would cost in the region of £350 each. A further £150 was allocated for the construction of the engine house and the erection of the timber winding frames sited at the top of the incline and on the tramroad bridge. A traditional straight linked chain was purchased for £100 and when installed, towards the end of May 1803, the plane was ready for business.

The inclined plane didn't quite perform as well as anticipated. Even Cartwright's beefed up specification for the engine was barely sufficient to cope with the tonnage it was asked to haul. The chain took nine minutes to complete one revolution and the waggons were attached at equal intervals enabling six to be raised up the incline for each revolution. The same number of descending waggons were lowered in the somewhat shorter time of six minutes. In 1822 the engine was upgraded to try and speed up the ascent.

A tremendous strain was placed upon the chain each and every time it was called upon to haul the waggons, which resulted in it stretching. After three and a half years it was found to have increased its length by one sixth. The chain, of course, could not go on stretching forever and when its limit was reached a catastrophe quickly followed.

The Preston Chronicle reported a terrible accident which occurred in 1826. The article implied that this type of accident was a regular occurrence and that as long as the canal company compensated the unfortunate victims, the situation was acceptable.

The Preston Pilot which also reported the incident was not so obliging, and laid the blame for the accident firmly at the door of the canal company. They ended their report by challenging the company to take steps to prevent a recurrence.

The reporter's protestations presumably struck home. A photograph

> **Accident At The Railway:–**
>
> On Tuesday morning last, about 10 o'clock. an accident happened on the Rail Road, by the breaking of the chain, used to drag the waggons up the inclined plane, at Avenham, in this town. John Roberts, one of the persons who is employed in conveying coals from the south to the north branch of the Lancaster Canal, had just disengaged his horses from the waggons, at the bottom of the hill, at the time when the last waggon of the person who preceded him, had nearly reached the summit. At this juncture the chain broke, the waggon descended with such dreadful velocity, that the railing proved insufficient to keep it in its regular track, and in its course it bore down on both of Roberts' horses, forced its way through the battlements of the bridge and fell into the river below. One of the horses afterwards rolled into the river and was so much injured that the owner caused it to be immediately stuck, as the bruises it had received added to the two broken limbs, rendered a cure impracticable. The other had a leg nearly severed from its body, and was otherwise so much bruised as to occasion almost instant death. The Lancaster Canal Company, according to their generous practice on similar occasions, it is expected will make good the loss thus sustained by the poor waggoner.
>
> *Preston Chronical October 7th 1826*

taken of the incline around the year 1869 clearly shows the garden referred too, laid out with stone setts and flags to facilitate the safe passage of the horses.

Given the poor quality of iron available at that time, the steepness of the incline and the heavy loads imposed on the chain, it is not surprising that the Avenham Incline was the scene of frequent accidents involving damage to property and injury or even death of men and beasts throughout the life of the tramroad.

> Shocking Accident.
>
> Some of our country readers may not be aware that the laden coal and other waggons which travel on the rail-road from the Summit to this town, are drawn up a very steep ascent on the Preston side of the Ribble, by the machinery of a steam-engine at the top of the hill. For this purpose, the horses are of course taken out, and the power of the engine generally applied to the draught of several waggons at a time, the last of the set being attached to the draught-chain when the first has nearly gained the top of the hill. On Tuesday morning last, two fine horses, just released from a set of waggons which had arrived at the foot of the brow were, as customary, slowly proceeding upwards, when the chain unluckily snapped, and two coal laden waggons which had nearly attained the summit, retrograding with dreadful violence, came in contact with the two poor animals, one of which was crushed to death on the spot while the other was hurried over the bridge into the river, with one of the vehicles. Every assistance was on hand to help the unfortunate beast out of the water which was only about a foot deep where it lay, but it wa found to be injured beyond all hope of recovery, and in mercy its throat was immediately cut.
>
> As the place at which this accident occurred is now become a thoroughfare for the public, we think it our duty in their behalf, to suggest to the Canal Company an increase of width on the road in question, by which a protected passage on one side for horses and passengers only. Such a space could easily be taken from the Company's garden on the right, and we trust that such an improvement will not be deferred till necessity shall be pressed by a catastrophe more serious than the one we have related.
>
> *Preston Pilot*

Various proposals were made over the years to improve or remove the Avenham Inclined Plane but all failed. As the various elements of the plane wore out or broke down they were replaced or repaired at minimal cost, but in 1858, as the tramroad neared the end of its working life, £120 had to be found to replace the boiler. Six years later the engine hauled its final train of waggons and in 1869 the engine house was demolished.

Whilst the tramroad was in operation, the footpath alongside the river passed beneath the tramroad bridge but some time after its closure the path was diverted to cross part way up the slope before diving down to continue its journey to Frenchwood at low level.

Nothing now remains of the engine house and its two small reservoirs. The site is now occupied by the Belvedere which was removed there in 1873 from Miller Park to

## The Main Features of the Tramroad

The Tram Bridge and Winding House – 1850.
Looking East along the public footpath which originally passed beneath the bridge.
(*Harris Ref. Lib.*)

make way for the Earl of Derby's Statue. As for the inclined plane, this too has long since vanished and the slope now forms part of the network of footpaths meandering through the park.

### Tramroad Bridge

The timber bridge straddling the Ribble at Avenham was thought a poor substitute for the magnificent stone aqueduct which was initially envisaged to carry the canal across the river at that point. However, although utilitarian in its design, it served the purpose for which it was originally intended and then went on to serve the public as a footbridge for many years after.

Early in 1802 William Cartwright turned his attention towards the crossing of the River Ribble. The lack of finances decreed that the 'temporary' bridge would have to be constructed as cheaply as possible and Cartwright would have expended little of his creative talents in designing the simple trestle type structure.

On 5 March Cartwright reported to Gregson that 4,000ft of deal timber had been purchased at Liverpool ready to commence the framing out of the bridge the following week.

The site chosen for the crossing was known locally as the stone delph, where the river had been made artificially deeper by the extraction of red sandstone from its bed for use in building the steeple for the parish church. In fact the sandstone proved too soft for its purpose and the steeple had to be rebuilt with a more durable type of rock. Whether the depth of the delph or the softness of the bed rock proved a difficulty during the erection of the bridge is not known, but whatever the problems, they seem to have been overcome without due difficulty for within three months the bridge was complete and awaiting its coat of preservative treatment which was to cost £200.

The finished bridge was described in 1821 as being 'supported by strong wooden mainstays, inserted in the bed of the river, and is railed on each side, measuring 135 yards long by 4 yards broad.'

Apart from the occasional damage caused by waggons careering back down the incline whenever the chain snapped, the bridge required only routine maintenance. However, as time passed, the weight of traffic it was asked to carry, and more particularly the regular buffeting the supports received from the turbulent Ribble, began to take their toll. By the 1830s more serious repairs were needed but canal company policy dictated that as little as possible was expended on the upkeep of the bridge in the anticipation that it would be rendered obsolete when the aqueduct could be afforded.

Inevitably the coming of the railways made the construction of an aqueduct a futile exercise, and in 1837 the Bolton & Preston Railway Company became the owners of the timber bridge when they purchased the tramroad as a way of entering Preston.

By this time the bridge supports were in a dangerous condition and the railway company was compelled, under the agreement made with the canal company, to replace them in order to maintain the safe passage of the tramroad traffic. Thereafter the railway company adopted their predecessor's attitude to the bridge and twenty years later it had again become unstable. As a result of various amalgamations, the Northern Union Railway Company were now the reluctant owners, and their engineers asked for the sum of £1,500 to provide a replacement. The money was not forthcoming, and it was recorded the following year that 'the bridge has already stood longer than the term originally intended and is at present in so very dangerous a condition that the footway over it is stopped during floods'. A photograph, taken about this time, shows intermediate supports installed between the main supports in an effort to stabilise the structure.

In 1862 the last coal waggon trundled over the groaning bridge, after which, only pedestrians were allowed to cross. Ten years later, the Preston Corporation had come to look on the bridge, together with the pleasant walk across the flood plain which the tramroad provided, as an amenity for the community and decided to acquire it.

On the 17 July 1872 the tramroad between Avenham and Carr Wood, including the bridge, became the property of the corporation. In return, the railway company were given Syke Road which ran from Garden Street via a tunnel under the southern end of the railway station to Waltons Parade. In order to maintain their ownership rights on the tramroad, the corporation was compelled to close it for one day each year.

With the intervention of the Preston Corporation, the future of the tramroad bridge was secured. Photographs taken after its change of ownership show the bridge to be in good order, no doubt as the result of heavy investment from the public purse.

*The Main Features of the Tramroad*

The Tram Bridge – 1860s.
On its last legs. Taken from the south bank looking up the Avenham Incline.
(*Harris Ref. Lib.*)

The Tram Bridge – 1902.
Looking in fine fettle, following some tender loving care lavished upon it by the corporation.
(*F.Harmann – J.Garlington*)

*The Old Tram Road*

In 1936 torrential rainfall caused the Ribble to flood, and the bridge was almost swept away when one of the central supports was struck by a hen house which had become embroiled in the boiling waters. Fortunately the bridge managed to ride the storm out and the corporation was able to effect the necessary repairs.

During the early stages of the second world war, invasion by Germany was seen as a genuine threat and the corporation, determined to make the passage of Hitlers tanks through Preston as onerous as possible, ordered the bridge decking to be removed.

With the ending of the war the decking was returned to its rightful place and the people of Preston could once again perambulate across the footbridge on their way to the pleasant tree lined walkway which the old tramroad now afforded.

Eventually, the temporary timber trestle bridge which had stood for over one hundred and sixty years became too costly to repair and a new structure was erected using the new wonder material, concrete. Fortunately the sound principles of the original structure were incorporated in the new, and the present bridge provides a good representation of the scene in 1802.

Tram Bridge Minus Timber Decking – 1946.
For the duration of the Second World War the timber decking was removed form the bridge in order to retard any possible German advance. (*Harris Museum*)

## *Fishergate Tunnel*

It had been perceived from the outset that Fishergate would present a natural barrier to the progression of the canal through Preston. The difference in level between the canal and the highway decreed that a tunnel would have to be constructed.

## The Main Features of the Tramroad

In 1801 William Cartwright prepared a plan showing a typical cross section through the proposed tunnel. It was to be constructed of stone as a circular arch with 18ins walls and have a width of 20ft. The depth of the water to be carried is shown as 6ft with a height of 14ft between the surface of the water and the soffit of the tunnel. To one side, a 4ft 6in wide path is incorporated to enable horses and men to pass through.

When lack of funds forced the committee to embrace the tramroad as the means of crossing the Ribble valley, the question of the tunnel was reviewed.

No doubt the committee would have preferred to install Cartwright's tunnel as originally designed. The dimensions would have easily accommodated a dual tramroad and when cash was available to continue the canal, the tunnel could then serve its original purpose. Unfortunately, the immediate cash flow situation precluded this option and the committee reluctantly decided to construct the tunnel as cheaply as possible, making it of sufficient dimensions to accommodate a single track only. Presumably the tunnel was constructed in a similar fashion to that shown on Cartwright's plan but of scaled down dimensions.

Either side of the tunnel, the tramroad was laid in cutting with the earth being retained by substantial stone side walls. At the point where the ground rose too high to be retained safely the tunnel was started. As the tunnellers passed below Fishergate they encountered ground conditions which made the going both difficult and potentially dangerous. The deadly combination of sand and water which they encountered would have been a constant threat as it sought to engulf the works and the men at every opportunity. After 90yds of labouring under terrible conditions the navvies eventually emerged into the cutting at the opposite side of Fishergate.

The tunnel provided the only point where the tramroad was reduced to a single track, which meant that the plates would have to carry double the amount of traffic. To cope with the increased loading, great care was taken in selecting only the highest quality plates for the job.

In 1813 the members of the committee again considered the possibilities of extending the canal, and Thomas Fletcher provided them with a cost estimate. His estimate included a sum of £2,700 for

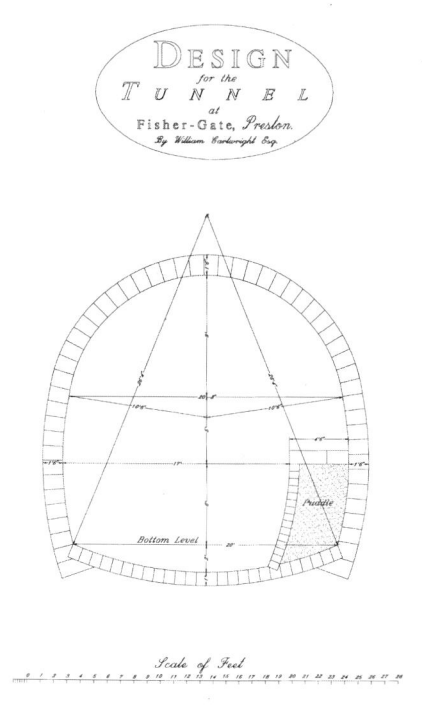

Design for a Tunnel Beneath Fishergate. Although this tunnel was designed to carry a canal, it could readily have been adapted to accommodate the Tramroad. (Based on drawing in *P.R.O.*)

75

*The Old Tram Road*

constructing a new tunnel at a rate of £30 per yd. The rate was high, as the tunnelling work was 'supposed to be through quick sand'. The total estimate was £160,537 5s 6d which when quoted to the committee, effectively guaranteed the future of the tramroad.

Despite various proposals over the years, none were implemented and the tunnel remained unaltered until the tramroad was closed. Five years later it was partially filled in to facilitate a road improvement and later still the London and North Western Railway Company, who by then owned the tunnel, decided to modify it. They enlarged the tunnel and turned the entrance parallel to Corporation Street to allow access from Charnley Street to their goods yard situated in Butler Street.

With the development of the Fishergate Centre the tunnel was again altered to facilitate access to the car park.

Today, none of the original tunnel exists although the line of the present underpass follows the route of the 1802 version.

## *Preston Basin*

At the start of 1801, the urban centre of Preston had yet to encompass the area of land to the north of Fishergate and west of Friargate. The dwellings which flanked those ancient highways backed onto pasture land which had for centuries been grazed by the town's livestock. This idyllic scene was about to be shattered in the name of progress by the imminent arrival of the country's most innovative form of transport. The fields offered the most favourable route for the Lancaster Canal to pass through Preston on its way to Wigan, being relatively central and containing few buildings of note.

Samuel Gregson busied himself with acquiring the land in advance of the works. He purchased all or part of the fields known as; Fishergate Meadow, Fishergate Lane Meadow, Great Field, Great Simpson Field, and The Nearer House of Correction Field which contained the recently obsolete Old House of Correction situated south of Marsh Lane and west of the proposed canal.

The canal had been cut as far as Spitalls Moss before the works were suspended pending a decision on how to cross the Ribble valley. The agreement to construct the tramroad signalled the resumption of works, and the canal once again began to creep southwards.

During the next two years a bridge was erected to carry the Old House of Correction Lane (Marsh Lane) and the cut reached its termination point, some 115yds short of Fishergate. The basin was formed at a point 40yds from the end of the main canal, almost at right angles to it and extended for 100yds in an easterly direction. The sides of the basin, together with the urban section of the canal were constructed of stone blocks or bricks laid in courses bedded on mortar and capped off with a stone coping.

As the spring of 1803 turned to summer, the Coal Road was nearing completion and the Limestone Road was well underway. The forming of the Preston Basin was lagging behind, and threatened the early opening of the tramroad. On 1 June The traders and boat owners who had applied for wharves informed the committee that in their opinion 'the said yards and wharfs are not in a fit state for letting'.

## The Main Features of the Tramroad

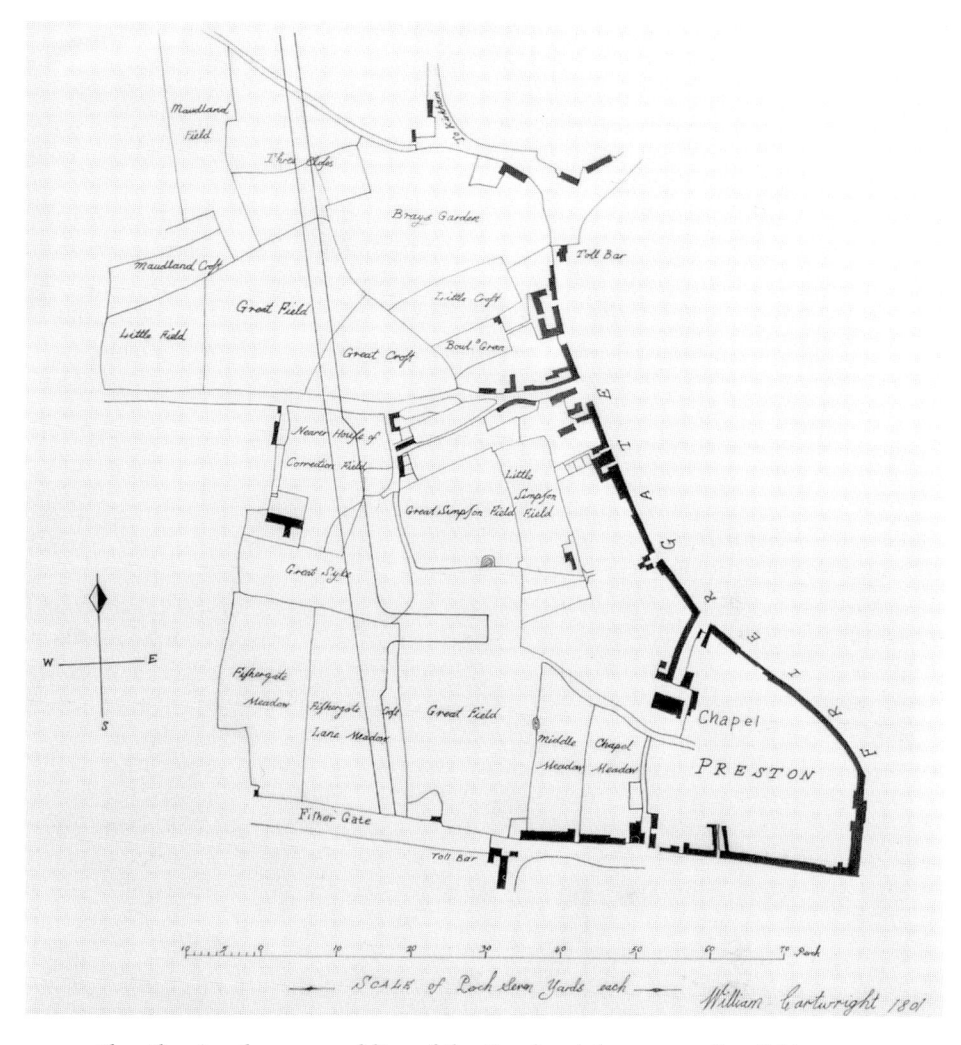

Plan Showing the proposed line of the Canal and the surrounding field names. Prepared by William Cartwright in 1801. Probably based on George Lang's map of 1774. (P.R.O.)

The latter half of the year saw a flurry of activity at the basin as the yards were paved out, and the iron plates forming the splice roads laid. The footings were being excavated for the £1,000 warehouse sited at the eastern end of the basin, and by November the coal hurreys were being erected over the end of the canal, sufficient to load three boats simultaneously. A plan of the coal hurreys shows timber staging extending 70ft over the end of the canal and supporting three tram lines. The decking was supported by 20ft long timber piles driven into the bed of the canal at 14ft centres longitudinally and 16ft 6ins transversly. The hurreys were set 8ft higher than the water

*The Old Tram Road*

level and the end wall of the canal was built up to suit. This enabled the waggons to run directly from the tramroad over the canal and discharge their cargo into the waiting barges positioned below.

Towards the end of February 1804 the 6ft high coursed stone walls separating the various yards were under construction and the final touches to the weigh bridge were in hand.

With the arrival of summer, the Preston Basin was ready to receive its first customers. The north side of the basin was designated a public wharf, and the south side was set out for the limestone trade, with the coal yards being sited closer to Fishergate. The limestone wharves were divided equally for the use of John Turner, The Earl of Balcarras, Thomas Dewhurst, and Mr K. McKenzie. These gentlemen also occupied the coal yards together with John Hodgson and Pearse Barker & Company. A single track entered each coal yard from the south, and the limestone wharves were served by a single track running along the edge of the basin.

The canal office was constructed alongside the tramroad close to the entrance to the Fishergate tunnel, and a group of buildings standing on the opposite side of the tracks housed William Bamford's Smith's Shop, John Cook's Joinery Shop and Mr McKenzie's Timber Yard.

All the original buildings and wharves were sited to the east of the canal around the basin area, but as trade on the canal increased, an area of land comprising some 35 acres to the west of the canal was gradually developed. By 1822, a complex arrangement of splice roads fanned out across the canal company's land, which extended as far as Pitt Street, serving a number of coal yards and factories including the company's own iron and brass foundry. The Preston Basin continued on in this

Preston Terminus of the Lancaster Canal.
Taken from an etching in Hewitson's *History of Preston* – 1883.
(S.B. based on etching by C.E. Shaw)

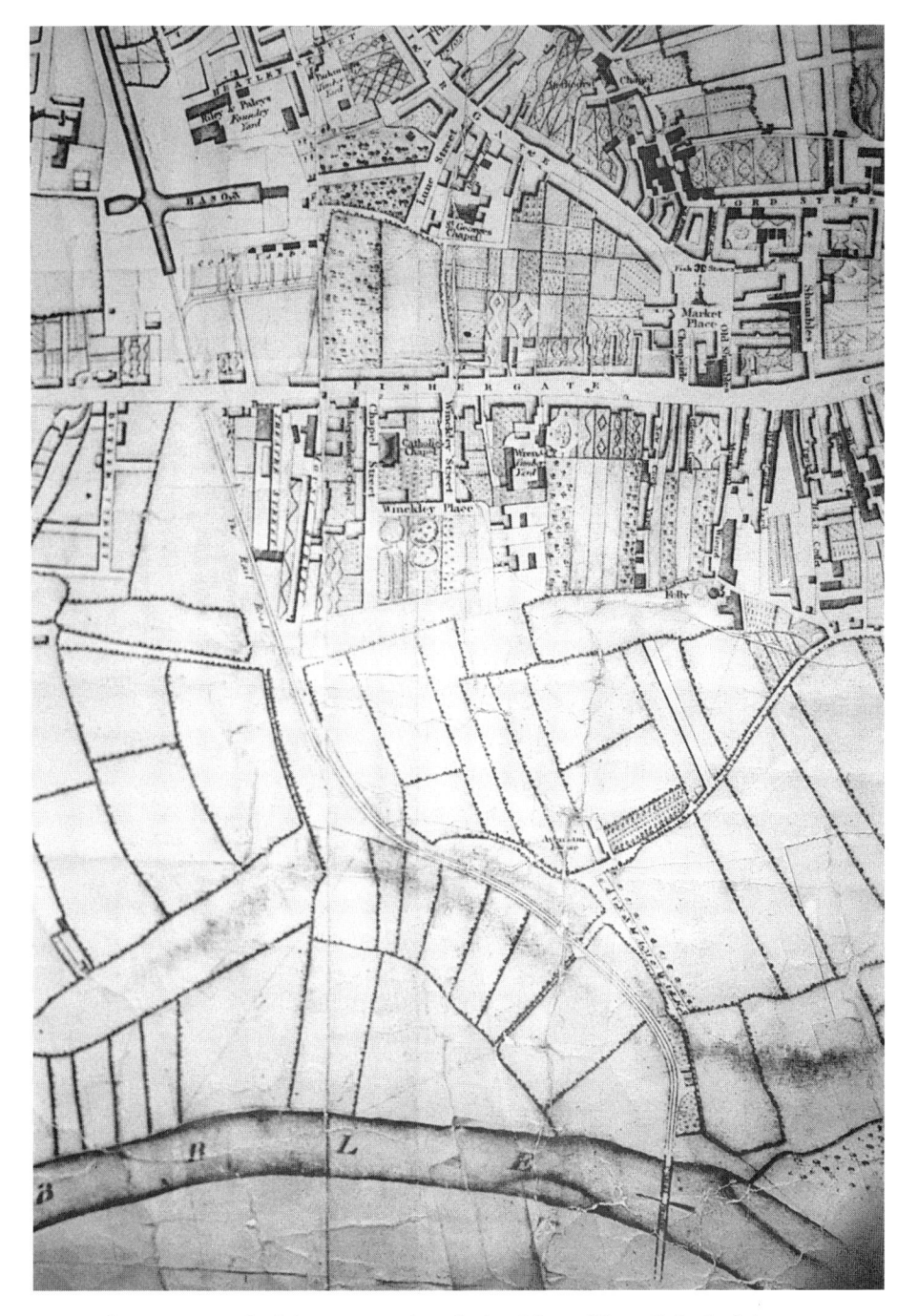

The Preston End of the Tramroad as depicted by William Shakeshaft in 1809.
(*Harris Ref. Lib.*)

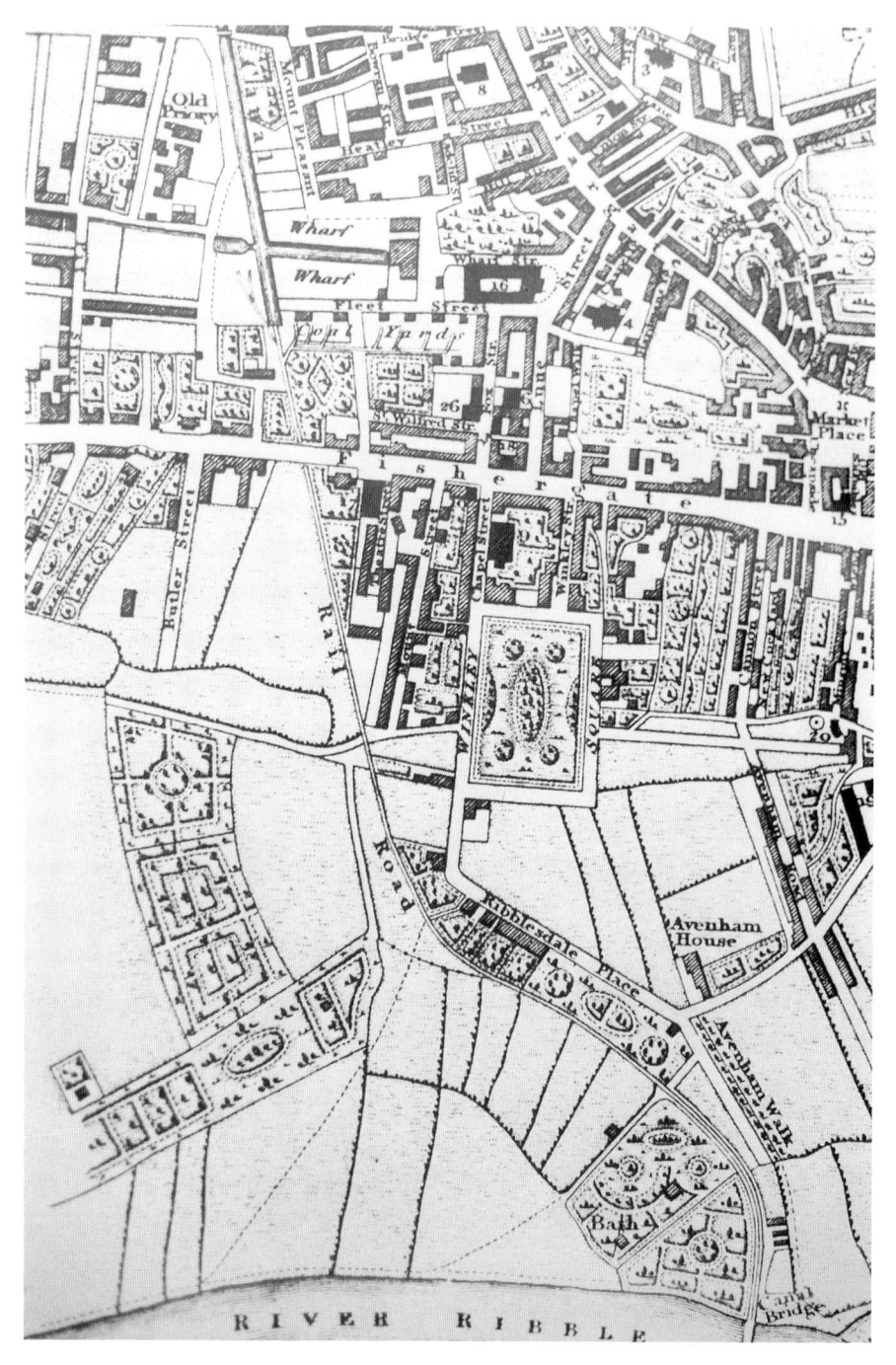

*The Old Tram Road*

The Preston End of the Tramroad as Baines saw it in 1824.
(*Harris Ref. Lib.*)

form for a further fifteen years when, inevitably, the all pervading railway knocked on the door.

For thirty five years, the North End of the Lancaster Canal enjoyed a monopoly over the transportation of heavy goods and materials to the country north of Preston. However its future looked bleak in 1837 when a bill was put before Parliament proposing to construct a railway between Preston and Lancaster. The canal company prepared a paper in opposition, highlighting the fact that the proposed line cut through the centre of their land north of Fishergate. The paper pointed out that 'Since 1822, an area of about Thirty-five acres, on the west side of the Canal, has been covered with Factories and other valuable Buildings'. It went on to state that if the new line were allowed it 'will deprive them of indispensable portion of their ground, and prevent the extension of conveniences and facilities, absolutely necessary in the formation of a Basin, Coal Yards, and Wharfs'.

It was argued, that on three previous occasions when railway companies sought to impinge on the canal company's land a clause was inserted 'restraining that Company from taking or entering upon any Wharfs, Lands, or other property of the Lancaster Canal Company, without their consent'.

The Lancaster Company had no doubt resigned itself to the inevitable competition that the railway would bring, and sought to get the best deal out of the situation that they could. In any event, Lord Stanley was able to push the bill through Parliament with little difficulty and the required land was purchased. The Lancaster & Preston Junction Railway was duly opened on 25 June 1840.

The Southern End of the Preston Basin – 1938.
Immediately beyond the railway waggons crossing the end of the canal, the Tramroad commenced its journey Southwards to Walton Summit, first passing under the buildings standing on Fishergate which form the horizon. (*Harris Ref. Lib.*)

*The Old Tram Road*

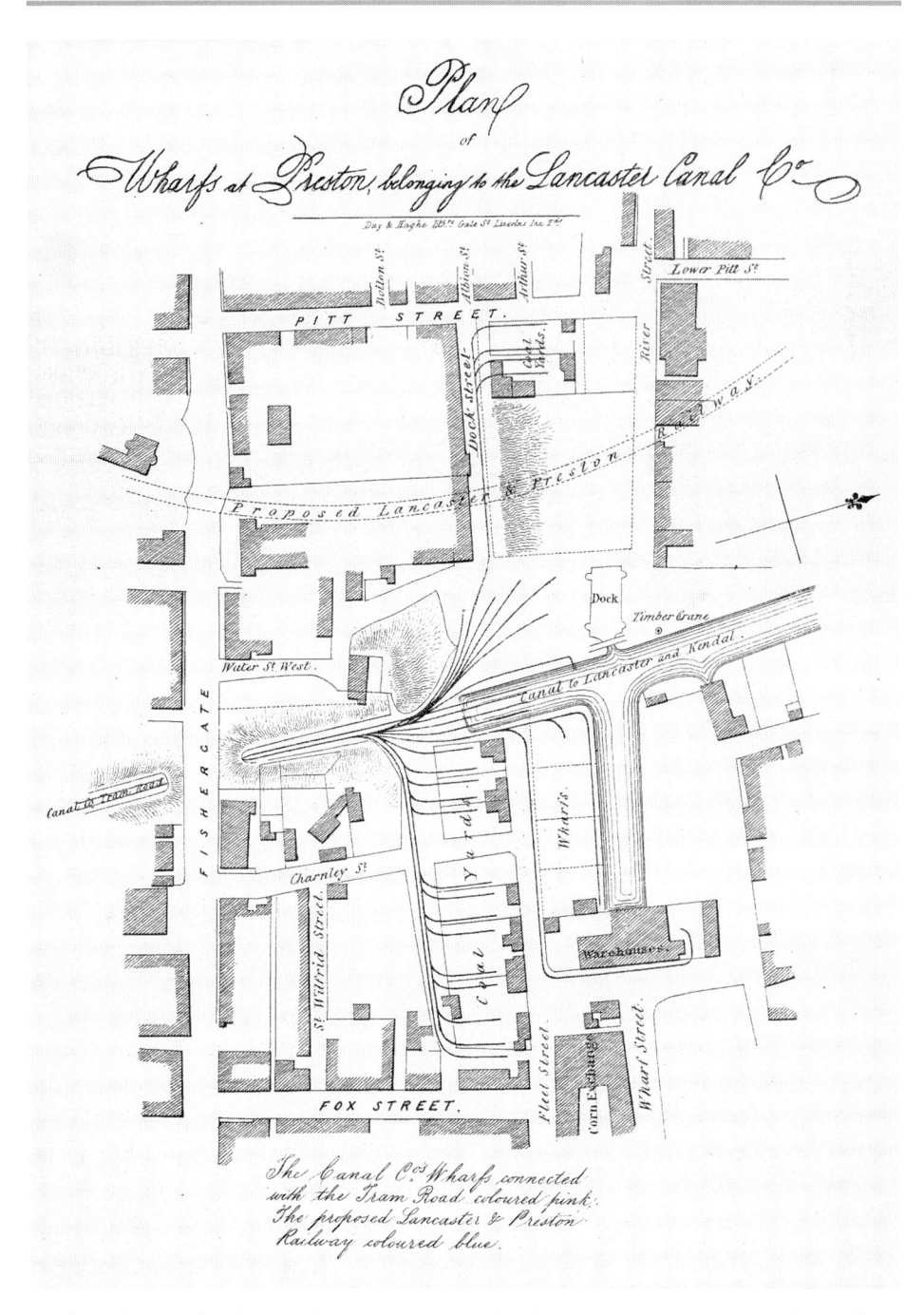

Plan submitted by the Canal Co. in 1837 opposing the Lancaster & Preston Railway Bill. (L.R.O.)

*The Main Features of the Tramroad*

Preston Basin.
The goods warehouse straddles the end of the eastern leg of the basin. The canal is in a dilapidated state awaiting infilling. The Aldi superstore currently occupies the site. (*Harris Ref. Lib.*)

The Ordnance Survey map for 1847 shows the Lancaster & Preston Railway had become part of the London & North Western. The railway seems to have overwhelmed the canal basin, with sidings reaching into every corner and crossing the canal at several points. The dry dock sited opposite the basin has been filled in and coal yards dominate the canal wharves south of Marsh Lane. The railway sidings are punctuated at frequent intervals by small turn-tables which allowed individual waggons to access sidings laid at 90 degrees to cross the canal. A drawbridge was constructed to carry the track across to the other side of the canal whilst at the same time allowing the free passage of barges.

As the trade on the tramroad declined, the railway took over the canal basin. By 1881 the tram lines had been removed and the end of the canal filled in to enable more railway sidings to be laid to the south of the basin. The canal continued its liaison with the railway for a further sixty six years but eventually bowed to the faster and increasingly more competitive road and rail transport. The canal finally ceased to trade in 1947 and was gradually filled in over the years as parts of it were sold off for redevelopment. The basin area was acquired by Dutton Forshaw who erected a car showroom on the site of the old warehouse.

At the time of writing, the Dutton Forshaw's building has been demolished in order to erect a new Aldi Superstore. The cellar walls of the old warehouse were briefly

83

## The Old Tram Road

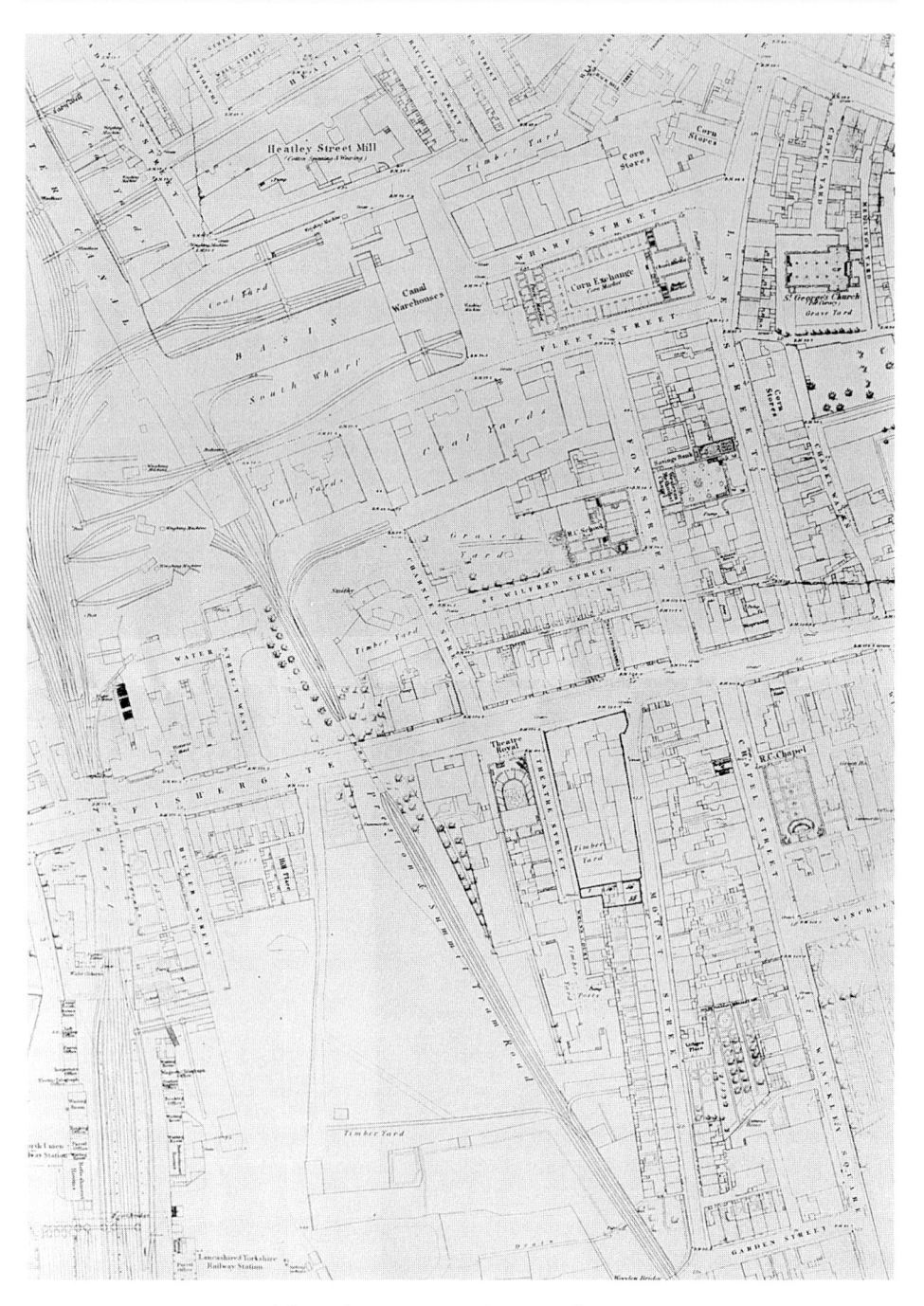

Tramroad from the Preston Basin to Garden Street – 1847.
The lines to the top and left of the map are part of the railway network. (O.S.)

revealed as the work progressed but have now again vanished, perhaps to reappear in another century. The car park to Railtrack's Ladywell house straddles the former canal up to Marsh Lane, with the offices occupying the former coal yards to the east of the canal. As for the southern tip of the canal and the tramroad to the north of Fishergate, their remains, if any, lie beneath the recently extended ring road.

## *Working the Road*

The Canal Company itself, oiled and maintained the wheels and axles of their waggons but it was up to the trader to ensure that the body of the cart was kept in good order. For those traders electing to use their own waggons, the company ordered that:

> the waggons of each trader shall be distinguished and marked by a letter and number on each side painted upon Tin or Iron, the plate for which shall be provided by the Canal Company and kept in repair and legible by the Trader.

On 3 July 1804 the company published a scale of charges to be made on the various materials likely to be waggoned across the tramroad:

> Upon all Coal, Cannel Coal and Cinders which shall be carried or pass upon and along the Rail Road from Walton Summit to Bamber Bridge a Tonnage Duty shall be paid of four pence per Ton (of one hundred and twelve pounds to the hundredweight and twenty of such hundreds to the Ton). From Walton Summit to Toad (Todd) Lane a Tonnage Duty shall be paid of six pence per Ton of the like weight. From Walton Summit to Penwortham a Tonnage Duty shall be paid of eight pence per Ton of the like weight. From Walton Summit to Preston Tonnage Duty shall be paid of one shilling per Ton of the like weight.

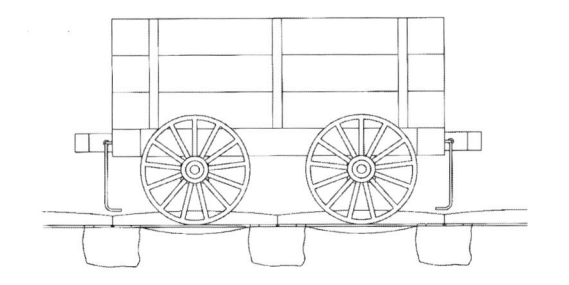

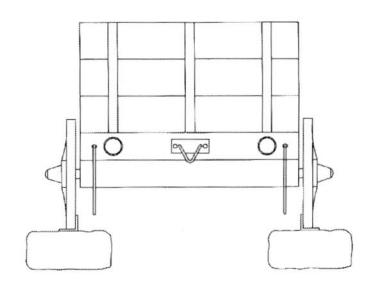

SIDE VIEW OF WAGGON      END VIEW OF WAGGON

Tramroad Waggon.
(S.B.)

## The Old Tram Road

A standard charge of 4*d* for the full length of the tramroad was levied:

upon all Coal, Slack, Limestone, Salt ores, Salt rock, Bricks, Stone Flags, Iron Stone, Black Bass, Iron, Cinders, Gravel, Sand, Clay Marl, and Manure Lime, Bar Iron, Cast Iron, and Pig Iron', and similarly 1*s* per ton 'upon all Slate Timber Drying Wood and all goods wares merchandise and commodities'.

When the waggons were fully laden to their 2 ton limit, it was found that they were too heavy, causing the primitive cast iron rails to buckle and break. After suffering the problem for nearly four years, the company decided to impose a limit of 1 ton per truck to prevent further damage: 'it has been found by experience that the quantity of two Tons carried in any Waggon at one time is too great, and very injurious to the Rail Road.' This move incensed the waggon drivers for they now had to make many more journeys to move the same tonnage of coal and limestone and they demanded a 25% increase in their wages. This in turn lead the traders to make representations to the company in an effort to have the new limit abolished. The arguments ran on for a further four years before the canal company was persuaded to make a concession: 'the extension of the weight to be carried in one Waggon to twenty five hundredweight will not materially injure the Rail – road, but will be a considerable benefit to the Traders.'

The waggon drivers were known as 'halers' (hauliers in modern spelling) and were employed by the traders to drive the teams of 2 or 3 horses pulling trains of 6 small or 4 large waggons loaded with the various cargoes between the two ends of the canal.

A typical scene at the Walton Summit Weighbridge House situated on Gough Line.
(S.B.)

# Working the Road

The job did not stop for the weather and the halers were expected to keep on working through, at times, atrocious conditions, sometimes walking, sometimes riding, urging on the tired horses, negotiating the three inclines and dealing with any derailments; it was not a job for the faint hearted.

After six months experience of operating the tramroad, the company realised that a set of rules, backed up by suitable fines, would be needed, otherwise chaos would reign. At a committee meeting held on 1 January 1805 it was resolved that:

> Any person or persons using or having any Waggon or Waggons upon the rail way belonging to the Company – shall wilfully or negligently permit or suffer such waggon or waggons, to obstruct or hinder the general and regular passage of the said rail way – he or they so offending shall forfeit and pay to the said Company the sum of five shillings for every such offence.

If the waggons were not moved immediately then the offender was fined a further 10s and recharged the cost of the company removing them.

It was essential that the waggons were not overloaded and the waggoners were fined 1s for every hundred weight over the 2 ton maximum allowed. To protect the horses, no more than four large or six small waggons were allowed to be linked together and 5s would be forfeited for each waggon over.

The Avenham incline was a potentially dangerous place to be, and in order to

Sketch of the Tram Bridge as it may have looked when in use.
(S.B.)

## The Old Tram Road

minimise the damage and injury which might occur as a result of the chain breaking, a rule was imposed to prevent horses and waggons approaching the incline whilst the preceding train was being hauled up the slope:

> if any person or persons using or having any Waggons upon the said rail way coming from the south shall enter upon the bridge crossing the river Ribble before the last Waggon of the team going before shall be hooked or fastened into the chain upon the inclined plane, he or they shall forfeit and pay to the said Company the sum of five shillings.

The final rule agreed upon at the meeting was directed at persons engaged in fly tipping. If the culprits were caught, a fine of 5s was to be imposed, together with the cost of moving the offending material. Probably due to the rough usage both the rails and the waggons were subjected to, derailments occurred frequently, whereupon the haler was obliged, under canal regulations, to stop the train and to lever the derailed waggon back onto the rails using an iron bar. However this procedure wasted time and required a lot of effort on behalf of the haler. As a result, the poor horses were often used to pull the waggons back on course, to the detriment of the rail flanges. Even worse, the trains just carried on going with the derailed waggon bumping along the stone sleepers causing further damage and sometimes turning over. On 6 January 1807 the company devised a system of fines to be levied against any persons mistreating the rails.

> Whereas several persons make a practice of crossing the Rail Ways with Waggons at various places not set out for that purpose to the great injury of same.
> Resolved that a fine of five shillings for each offence shall be paid for the driver of every Waggon which shall cross the Rail way except at such places where shunts or shunning ways are provided.
> And whereas drivers Waggoners hook their horses to their Waggons which from any cause have gotten out of the regular Road, and by the power of their horses draw the same again into the Road to the great injury of the same.
> Resolved that a fine of five shillings for each offence shall be paid by the Driver of every Waggon who shall not lift his Waggon by means of Levers into and upon the Rail Road when the same shall by accident or otherwise be thrown out of the regular course of the Road.

The company's rules were frequently added to and amended as experience dictated. In 1814 it was resolved that:

> a fine of five shillings shall be paid by the driver of any Waggon who shall continue to draw a Waggon or Waggons along or across the Road after the wheels of such Waggon or Waggons shall have gotten off the Cast Iron Plates.

Another trick of the halers was to fall asleep in the waggon leaving the horses unattended, and a bylaw was introduced in 1828 prohibiting this potentially hazardous practice.

The tramroad was the scene of many accidents of varying severity during its unexpectedly long life. One of the most tragic occurred in January 1809 when a waggon ran over a haler.

In 1813 the estimated cost of replacing the tramroad with a canal had risen to £160,537 and the committee, instead, opted to spend the lesser sum of £98,095 on extending the canal northwards through to Kendal. By this time the tramroad was booming, with nineteen teams making the round trip between the Summit and Preston twice daily.

By 1817 traffic on the tramroad had increased to such an extent that the traders were compelled to make representations about the delays being experienced at the inclines. The company responded by diverting the line at Penwortham to allow the horses to negotiate the slacker gradient without assistance, followed in 1822 by the installation of a more powerful engine at Avenham which was purchased second hand for £240.

> A shocking accident happened last week in Walton, on the rail-road of the Lancaster Canal; – The driver of some coal waggons, coming on the rail-road in the evening, with several loaded waggons, by some means or other was thrown down across the road the waggons were upon, and, dreadful to relate, they passed over him, nearly severing him in pieces, and leaving him an object to, shocking for description. The unfortunate man, we are informed, has left a large family to lament his untimely fate.

The last haler to work on the Walton Summit to Preston Basin Tramroad was a man by the name of John Proctor who was still living in Preston in 1883. He walked the line for thirty two years, making the return journey twice a day, a distance of twenty miles. It was once estimated that he had travelled 199,000 miles walking or riding during the course of his working life. In the early part of his career he must have done more walking than riding for he needed his clogs to be resoled at the end of every week.

A John Proctor appears in the 'List of Persons Entitled to Vote at the Election of Members for the Borough Council of Preston' for 1831 where his occupation is described as 'Waggoner' and his address as no. 4 Butler Street.

## Attempts to Replace the Tramroad

Seven years after the tramroad came into operation, the Lancaster contingent were still optimistic that its life-span would be short: 'the rail-road makes a good temporary communication between the North and South parts of the canal until the lockage in that part is complete.'

In 1813 Thomas Fletcher, who had been with the company for seventeen years, was asked to prepare an estimate of cost for replacing the tramroad with a canal. He estimated that the provision of a canal 14ft wide at the bottom and 30ft wide at the surface, some 4 miles and 5 furlongs in length would cost in the region of £160,000 and submitted an itemised breakdown for the benefit of the committee.

At least the proprietors now knew how much money needed to be raised, and every avenue was explored in an attempt to finance the scheme.

*The Old Tram Road*

### Thomas Fletcher's Estimate for Replacing the Tramroad (1813)

| | £ | s | d |
|---|---:|---:|---:|
| Beginning at Preston | | | |
| N.B. The whole of the cutting contained in the line of the canal is included and allowed for in the Ribble embankment. | | | |
| To tunnelling at Fishergate Road (supposed to be through quicksand) 90 yards @ £30 | 2700 | 0 | 0 |
| To cutting and banking the Syke Valley etc. | 70 | 2 | 0 |
| To building an aqueduct of three arches over the Ribble | 21094 | 0 | 0 |
| To the Ribble embankment 1060177 cub yds @ 1s | 53008 | 17 | 0 |
| To embanking the ends of the valley 28656 cub yds @ 7d | 835 | 16 | 0 |
| | 53844 | 13 | |
| To allow for the shrinking of the earth in the embankment ⅕ | 10768 | 18 | |
| | £64613 | 11s | 0d |
| N.B. the cutting of the south side of the valley to the head of the sixth lock is included in the expence for forming the Ribble Embankment. | | | |
| To cutting the canal and lock pits, from the sixth lock to the Summit level; also banking on the back of the locks | 3291 | 4 | 6 |
| To puddling and lining the Ribble Embankment | 635 | 5 | 0 |
| To puddling the locks, and the necessary side puddles | 483 | 0 | 0 |
| To gravelling and fencing off the towing paths, also resoiling the banks | 1384 | 19 | 0 |
| To culverts and valve trunks | 300 | 0 | 0 |
| To building 7 bridges 12ft within; 10 ditto, 9ft within and one upon the turnpike road at Bamber Bridge | 4010 | 0 | 0 |
| To an aqueduct bridge under the Ribble Embankment | 1000 | 0 | 0 |
| To 229 feet of lockage @ £160 per foot | 36640 | 0 | 0 |
| | 136852 | 1 | 6 |
| To casual and supervisal expenses, 10% on the above | 13685 | 4 | 0 |
| | 150537 | 5 | 6 |
| To land and damages | 10000 | 0 | 0 |
| Length 4 miles and 5 furlongs    Total | 160537 | 5 | 6 |

By 1825 the optimism had faded somewhat and Baines reflects the mood of frustration in his *History of Lancashire*:

> When the company determined to adopt this measure, the town of Preston was considered inferior to Lancaster, and did not contain more than 10,000 inhabitants but the population has now increased to upwards of 30,000 and the consumption of coal for steam engines has increased in a double ratio to the population.

He went on to outline the benefits that Preston was missing out on due to the continued use of the tramroad:

> an additional source of wealth will open upon this much favoured town with the replacement of the Tramway by an Aqueduct, since in addition to the loss, inconvenience and delay of unloading and reloading, coal and lime the carriage of corn and other agricultural produce, as well as of iron work, cotton wool, manufactured goods and general merchandise is nearly, if not altogether lost to this canal company and the advantage of the inland navigation so far lost to the publick.

Two years later, Twyford and Wilson, a firm of surveyors and civil engineers based in Manchester, prepared a promising scheme to couple the North End of the canal to the Leeds & Liverpool by way of the Douglas Navigation, crossing the Ribble at Freckleton via."booms" and then locking up to the Lancaster at Salwick.

The following report dated 26 October 1827 outlining the scheme was submitted to a public meeting for debate:

> we turned our attention to the Douglas Navigation by which a communication is already affected between the Leeds and Liverpool and the Ribble. From the mouth of the Douglas we propose to cross the Ribble to Freckleton, on its opposite bank, conveying the Vessels across by the common method of hauling, and the horses by means of Booms consisting of 3inch planks, firmly bolted down to beams, and moored with chains so disposed that each part of the boom will rise and fall with the tide. Upon this Boom lights may be exhibited; which will at once serve to prevent accidents and to distinguish the channel during the night, or dense fogs. In the middle of the river, two channels are formed by a sandbank on which we would place two transport buoys which would serve to indicate these channels to vessels navigating the Ribble.
>
> Having by this expedient, and at trifling expense, crossed the Ribble to Freckleton, it will be necessary to rise from low water to the level of the Lancaster Canal, near to Salwick Hall, which does not exceed 79ft 4 inches and may be easily effected by 10 locks of 8ft rise each, and of the dimensions of 66ft by 15ft which are calculated for vessels drawing 5ft of water. Mr Rennie's plan, besides the extensive embankment, and gigantic Aqueduct with a considerable quantity of cutting between beginning and the end of the Railway, requiring no less than 229ft of lockage; so that by the plan now proposed, there is an immense saving both of money and time, independent of its superior local advantage.

The cost of the lockage was estimated at £7,600. The cost of cutting the canal from Freckleton to Thornton a distance of 8 miles 1540yds and the link to join the Lancaster Canal from Kirkham to Salwick, a further 2 miles 660yds, was £80,000.

Like all its predecessors, the scheme was rejected and the tramroad's immediate future was again secure.

## *Samuel Gregson*

Sometime during the 1830s, Samuel Gregson's son, Bryan Paget Gregson was taken on as his assistant. The appointment was questioned by some shareholders who wondered whether there was sufficient work to warrant an assistant, and why the clerk's son had been appointed to the post. It was also revealed at this time that Samuel Gregson was a partner in the firm that supplied coal for the Avenham winding engine at a price which was higher than other local suppliers. A special committee was set up to investigate the matter which, after considering all the facts, exonerated him from any allegations of malpractice. In order to prevent a recurrence of the unfortunate incident, Gregson agreed to cease trading with the company for the remainder of his tenure as clerk/secretary.

*The Old Tram Road*

Although Gregson's action might be looked on today with suspicion, it was not uncommon in the nineteenth century for engineers and administrators to invest in and supply materials to their undertaking, nor was it unusual for nepotism to be practiced. Perhaps the charges were brought by somebody who had a vested interest in seeing him dismissed.

Gregson's role in the canal company would equate to that of general manager today. He worked tirelessly in his efforts to, first build and then run the canal to the benefit of the shareholders. In doing so he gained the respect of the local community, which was amply demonstrated when on two occasions he was elected Mayor of Lancaster. He continued administering the affairs of the Lancaster Canal Company from the canal office in Queens Square, Lancaster until his retirement, whereupon his son took over the reigns.

Gregson lived out the remainder of his life in the nearby village of Caton. He died on 27 October 1846 at the ripe old age of 83, leaving an estate valued at £18,000.

An ornate marble memorial tablet is affixed to the chancel wall inside Lancaster Priory, sited adjacent to the castle:

> To the memory of Samuel Gregson of Lancaster and Caton esq. Formerly one of the Aldermen of this borough and mayor in 1817–18 and 1825–26. He was born at Lancaster 3 March 1763, and died at Caton 27 October 1846 in his 83rd year. His long life was distinguished by activity and zeal in promoting the prosperity of his native town; by uprightness of conduct; by gentleness of disposition and by the consistency of his Christian character.
>
> Here we have no continuing city, but we seek one to come. Heb. 13 v. 14

## *Attempts to Improve the Tramroad*

Meanwhile, Bryan Paget Gregson was destined to guide the canal company through the turbulent years of competition, with the various railway undertakings which would inexorably drain the lifeblood from the canal. He was well aware of the potential threat of the railways and sought to reduce their effect by staying one step ahead. In September 1827 he went on a spying mission, first to the Stockton & Darlington and then to the Bolton & Leigh Railways with a view to seeking out ways of improving the efficiency of the tramroad. Upon his return, he suggested that the tramroad waggons should be constructed with broader wheels attached directly to the axle. He also suggested the provision of brakes as a more efficient method of stopping the waggons than the 'lock chains' in use at the time.

As for the tramroad itself, it was proposed to enlarge the Fishergate tunnel to accommodate a dual track and to by-pass the Avenham incline by re-routing to avoid the steep slope. Had these suggestions been implemented the efficiency of the tramroad would have improved significantly. Unfortunately the committee, whilst no doubt appreciating the benefits of the proposal, thought it not worth the expense and rejected it.

By 1828 the techniques of manufacturing iron had improved sufficiently to allow a

## Attempts to Improve the Tramroad

9ft long plate to be developed, and Gregson sought to introduce these on the tramroad. An experimental length was ordered to be cast by Lyndsay & Co. of Preston which was subsequently laid down within the single track of the Fishergate Tunnel. The experiment proved successful and the western side of the Walton Summit incline was relaid with the new plates, which had the effect of enabling five fully laden waggons to be taken up where previously only two were possible.

By 1831, the Lancaster Canal Tramroad's very existence was directly threatened by the authorisation of the Preston & Wigan Railway. Gregson could see no future for the tramroad operating in competition with a parallel railway and proposed abandoning it and seeking amalgamation with the railway company. The committee however, would not entertain amalgamation at this stage, and so Gregson prepared a scheme to upgrade the tramroad to the status of railway which he estimated would cost in the region of £11,650.

The committee wanted a second opinion, and George Stephenson was engaged to look into the matter. He proposed two diversions and included four self acting inclines, whilst retaining the steam powered static winding engine at Avenham, all for the total sum of £11,894 18s.

Stephenson's proposals were never adopted and Gregson wrote disparagingly about his efforts:

> 'I cannot but consider Mr Stephenson's plan attended with many difficulties and inconveniences, not only in execution but even in operation'.

The tramroad was left to trundle along as before but it would not be long before it's existence would again be threatened.

Nine foot long tramplate
As techniques of iron manufacture improved, longer lengths of rail could be produced. The 9ft long rails were successfully tested in the Fishergate Tunnel. This example displayed in 1971 turned up on an allotment at Brownedge. (*G.Biddle*)

## Railways

The tramroad and steam engine were both born out of necessity in the coal fields of Britain: the tramroad to transport the coal, and the steam engine, initially, to pump ground water from the mines.

The depth to which early coal reserves could be extracted was restricted by the problem of ground water infiltrating and flooding the mines at a rate faster than it could be removed. The development of an efficient method of removing the water would be the key to unlock the vast wealth stored below.

The breakthrough came in 1712 when Thomas Newcomen constructed his atmospheric steam engine to pump water from a coal-mine at Dudley Castle. The static beam engine had massive proportions and consumed prodigious amounts of coal in order to achieve the power output required to pump water from the mine at a sufficient rate.

James Watt and Matthew Boulton developed Newcomen's idea further by adding a condenser and powering the piston with steam instead of air pressure. This modification allowed smaller beam engines to be constructed which were more frugal in their appetite for coal.

Most tramroads incorporated steep slopes which were negotiated using a combination of counter balancing weights and teams of horses. It wasn't long before Watt and Boulton, looking for other uses for their invention, hit upon the idea of positioning an engine at the top of an incline and using it to wind a drum with a rope attached to haul the heavy waggons up the slope with ease. Thus began the long and fruitful partnership between steam and rail which would ultimately transform the world.

Watt and Boulton persevered with their low pressure engine, endeavouring to increase power by introducing larger and larger cylinders, up to 10ft in diameter and more. This line of development was a long way from the type of small, light, high powered unit which would be needed to drive a locomotive. The steam engine developed little until Watt and Boulton's patent expired in 1800 allowing others to introduce fresh ideas to the invention.

For the continued development of the steam engine one has to look towards Devon and Cornwall where the copper and tin mining industry met with the same problems as the collieries but without the aid of unlimited, cheap, on site fuel to power the pumps. The motivation for the engineers in this area was to develop a steam engine to do the job using the least amount of coal possible. Richard Trevithick had constructed just such an engine ready for use upon the expiration of Watt and Boulton's monopoly. His engine worked on high pressure steam which allowed a much smaller cylinder to develop the same power and had the added benefit of a substantial reduction in fuel consumption, which made it ideal for use in the copper and tin mines.

It wasn't long before the substantially reduced proportions of the steam engine led engineers to thoughts of unshackling the beast from its traditional stationary role of winding cables to pull waggons along tracks. If the engine could be made light enough and powerful enough, then why not mount one on its own wheels and try pulling the waggons along behind.

# Railways

*Central Railway Station*

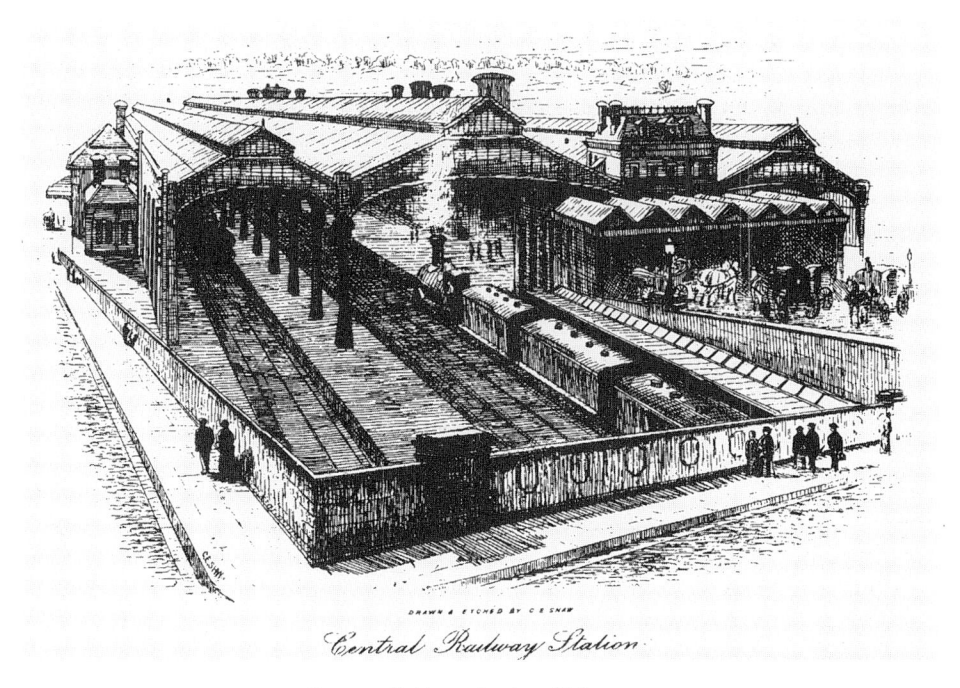

Preston Railway Station, Fishergate
Taken from an etching in Hewitson's *History of Preston* – 1883. (*C.E.Shaw*)

There followed thirty years of frenetic and diverse development which culminated in 1829 with the creation of Stephenson's Rocket, which was the first to embody all the principles of the modern steam powered locomotive and enabled the growth of the main line railway network.

The 1830s saw the formation of a number of railway companies, initially to fill the gaps in the transportation network where canals could not be economically constructed, and more latterly in direct competition to the canal companies themselves.

Preston was a key town in the development of railways along the western side of Britain, and many newly formed companies sought entry to the town from the south.

The first railway to connect with Preston was that opened by the North Union Railway Company in 1838, which in 1834 had absorbed the Preston & Wigan. The line crossed the Ribble at Miller Park and terminated in the town south of Fishergate, and today forms part of the main line between London and Glasgow.

In 1836 the Bolton & Preston Railway Company also sought access to Preston from the south and, unable to reach agreement to use part of the North Union, decided that the tramroad represented an easy, ready-made entry into the town. If an agreement could be reached, the need for lengthy and difficult negotiations with numerous land owners, the expense of land purchase and the cost of making good the connections between highways, watercourses and drains and the like which were inevitably severed when a new line was constructed, could be avoided.

## The Old Tram Road

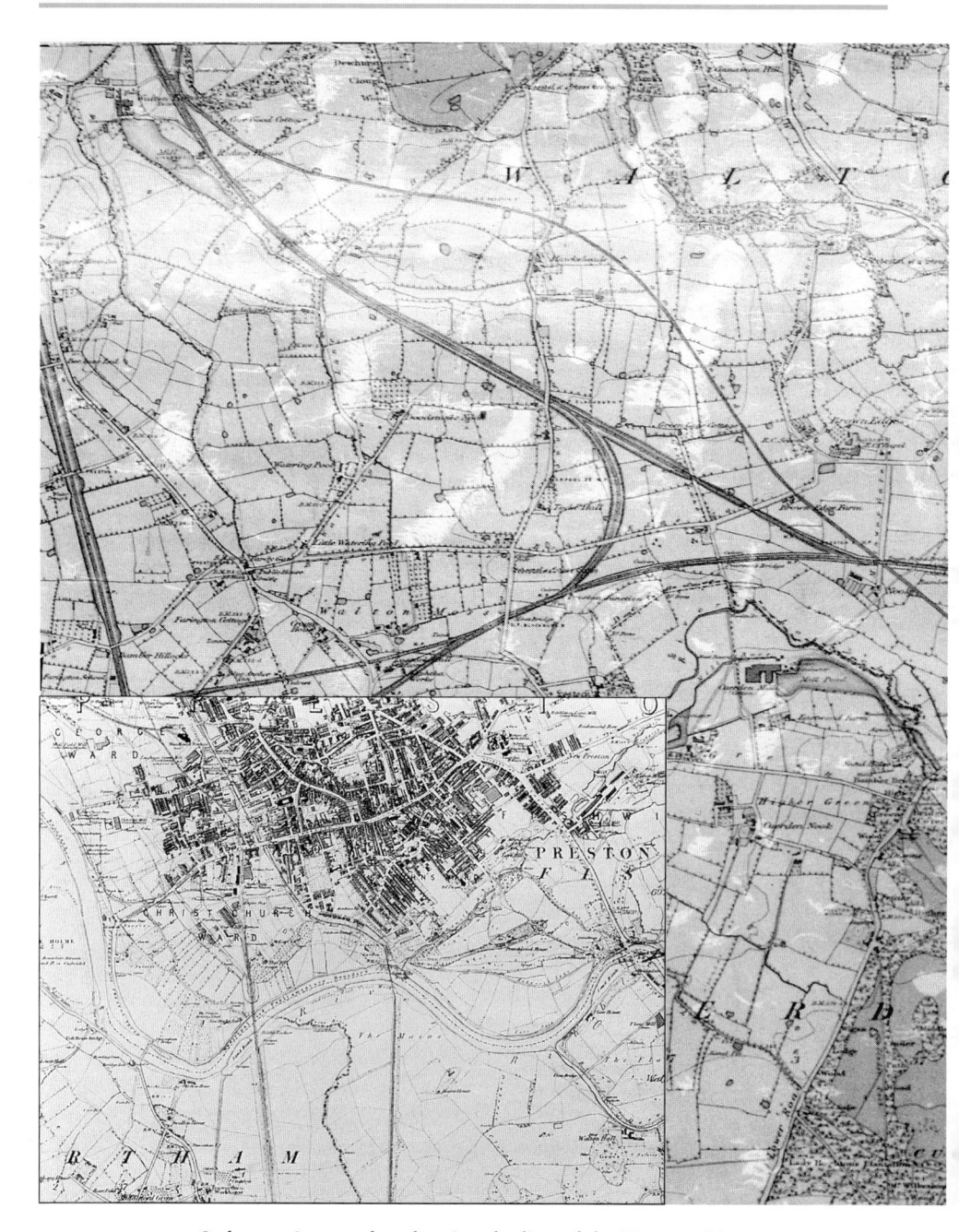

Ordnance Survey plan showing the line of the Tramroad in 1845.
This plan together with that on the following page shows the full length of the tramroad from north to south, the inset shows the Preston end.

*Railways*

Agreement was reached between the two companies on 27 January 1837 when the canal company leased the tramroad to the railway company in perpetuity. However the lease was not without its conditions which were subsequently incorporated in the Bolton & Preston Railway Act of 1837.

The Act specified that the new railway was to connect the two ends of the canal, for which purpose the canal company was to set aside a strip of land 10yds wide between Fishergate and the canal's 'graving dock' upon which the railway company was to construct and maintain in good repair, at their own expense, a twin track for the use of both companies. The South End of the canal was to be connected at Walton Summit or at any point to the south to be determined by the railway company, provided that, at their own expense, new and suitable wharfage was constructed. The railway company was empowered to incorporate any part of the tramroad into their line or to construct new as they saw fit, but with the proviso that they should 'make and keep open, and in good repair, clear of obstructions, hindrance or impediment, for the conveyance of coal, slack, goods, wares and merchandise, a free and open passage, by railway or tramroad'. The only other restrictions were, that the connections to the two ends of the canal should be completed by the time the main line was opened, and that during construction work the company was 'restrained and prohibited from breaking the surface of Fishergate Street in Preston'.

Incorporated in the deal was an agreement requiring the canal company to set aside 2,000 sq yds of their land to the north of Fishergate, adjacent to the proposed canal siding, to allow the railway company to construct a new station. For this privilege, a yearly rent was levied 'not exceeding two shillings for every superficial square yard' which was to be paid quarterly, beginning seven years after the passing of the Act.

The Act was subsequently passed and the tramroad, to all intents and purposes, became the property of the Bolton & Preston Railway Company.

The railway company got their entry into Preston, enough land to construct a station and the tolls payable for using the South End of the canal, except for the Leeds & Liverpool traffic.

The canal company got rid of an ageing tramroad constructed as a temporary expedient and therefore with little regard to life expectancy, which eventually would lead to ever more frequent and expensive repairs, and gained a fast and efficient connection between the two ends of the canal via the new locomotive worked railway, plus £8000 a year rent.

Even after signing the agreement with the canal company, the Bolton & Preston Company continued negotiations with the North Union, and on the 4 July 1838 a deal was struck whereby the Bolton & Preston were allowed to run over the North Union tracks and use their station.

As a result, the tramroad was never changed, altered or upgraded to the status of a railway and was instead left as an unwanted millstone around the neck of the Bolton & Preston Railway Company who decided, not unreasonably, to continue collecting the tolls whilst spending as little as possible on maintenance.

The canal company still needed the tramroad at this stage and were forced to negotiate an agreement with the railway company to ensure that they maintained the track properly. This cost the canal company £600 a year which was increased to £1000 following an agreement dated 6 September 1838.

## The Declining Years of the Tramroad

The tramroad bridge presented the railway company with their first expense, with its supports having been gradually worsening during the ownership of the canal company. The job could be put off no longer and minimal repairs were ordered and effected. It was at this stage that the railway company decided to replace all future broken cast iron plates with the recently developed and more durable wrought iron plates.

The railway company did tolerably well during its first year of tenure taking £10,000 in tolls and expending £9,000 on essential repairs and payment of the yearly rental. However, within ten years, this small profit was to turn into a £5,600 per year loss to the North Union Company, who had by then inherited the lease, when only £1,780 was taken in tolls.

The arrangement lasted for five years until the Bolton & Preston disputed the rates being charged by the North Union for the use of their line, whereupon they resurrected their plans to use the tramroad to enter Preston independently. This was in fact little more than a ploy devised to push the two companies towards amalgamation. The ploy had its desired effect and in 1844 the Bolton & Preston joined with the North Union which, in effect, ensured that the idea to turn the tramroad into a railway was shelved forever.

Shortly after the amalgamation, the North Union constructed the branch line, originally promised by the Bolton & Preston Company, to connect the North End of the canal at Preston Basin to the railway network.

With the creation of the branch line, the demise of the tramroad was inevitable. Preston became a railhead with coal arriving from the south via the railway where it was loaded into barges for its journey north on the canal.

Although the North Union Company adopted their predecessor's policy of expending as little money as possible on the

Cast Iron Boundary Posts. Installed to identify the extents of the North Union Railway Co.'s land ownership at Walton Summit. Stored at South Ribble Museum. (S.B. – 1998)

tramroad, they could not ignore their responsibilities with regard to essential maintenance. By 1847 the railway company, faced with the prospect of having to carry out major repairs to the tramroad bridge, asked the canal company to relax the conditions in the 1837 agreement and allow them to close the tramroad. The suggestion didn't suit the canal company's purposes at that time, and they insisted that the original agreement was adhered to, and the bridge was subsequently repaired. The scene was re-enacted again some nine years later when the bridge was found to be in danger of collapse. The North Union estimated the cost of a replacement at £1,500 but, after being refused the option of closure, decided to patch the bridge up sufficiently to enable it to last a few more years.

Charles Hardwick described the condition of the bridge as he saw it in 1857:

> The bridge has already stood longer than the term originally intended and is at present in so very dangerous a condition that the footway over it is stopped during floods.

Meanwhile, other areas of the tramroad infrastructure were suffering from the ageing process. The tramroad had taken a pounding every day for over half a century, and the plates were forever having to be replaced or realigned. The winding mechanisms were also a drain on resources, and in 1858 £120 had to be spent to buy a new boiler for the Avenham engine.

An article appeared in the Preston Guardian on 17 July 1858 describing the operation of the tramroad at that time:

> Mr Dewhurst has a couple of horses occasionally passing on the line, and so far as we are informed, is the only custom. This splendid railway normally employs four men, one an

Tram Bridge – 1860s.
A few intrepid promenaders risk life and limb on the dilapidated structure. (*Harris Museum*)

engine man, one to look after the line, one at the weighing machine and another somewhere else, though we expect they have not half work.

It was generally thought that the tramroad was kept open purely as a means of preventing the North Union Railway Company gaining a monopoly over the transportation of coal into Preston. In fact it was stipulated in the Bolton & Preston Railway Act that this length of tramroad had to remain open.

The corporation at this time had recently expended £3,000 on the purchase of land at Avenham in order to form a public park. Popular opinion was growing to rid the proposed park land of the unsightly tramroad, and one gentleman, who described himself as 'an old inhabitant' wrote to the Preston Guardian suggesting that 'the present abominable nuisance of clanking chains and unsightly smoking chimney' be got rid of, otherwise the park would be 'deteriorated by the perpetuation of so foul a nuisance'.

In 1873, the Guardian carried a retrospective article describing the suffering of the residents of Avenham Colonnade:

> Park-goers will recollect that the back doors of the houses in the Colonnade opened on the tramway and dismal enough was the arrangement. Abutting on a dirty road plentifully treated with all manner of refuse.

Although the tramroad was on its last legs, an Act obtained by Preston Corporation in May 1861 to construct a highway over the tracks demonstrated that the possibility of its being upgraded to the status of a railway had not altogether been discounted.

View over Avenham.
Painted before the Corporation formed the park ... The Tramroad bridge and engine house can be seen in the distance. (*Harris Ref. Lib.*)

*The Old Tram Road*

View over the Ribble Valley – taken from Avenham Colonnade.
Tramroad plates can be seen crossing the end of the Lane.

The corporation may in the construction or widening of the street leading from Ribblesdale Place to Avenham Park, carry or continue the same over the tramway. Provided that the bridge over the tramway shall be made so as to leave 7ft in the clear above the rails of such a bridge; but if the companies in whom the said tramroad is vested ever hereafter require to use the said tramway for locomotive engines, then such bridge shall be raised by the said corporation at their expense, to a height not exceeding 15ft in the clear above the rails for the whole length of such bridge.

The tramroad's days were indeed numbered. Its existence was inextricably tied to the fortunes of the canal company who, like others throughout the country, were fighting a losing battle against the all pervading and ever expanding railway network.

In January 1862, a team of horses set off to haul its waggons between Walton Summit and Preston Basin for the last time. Two years later, the Lancaster Canal Company, who at the outset had been forced to construct the tramroad due to lack of funds and had sought ever since to remove it, were finally able to wash their hands of it.

The Lancaster Canal Transfer Act, passed on 29 July 1864, enabled the canal company to lease in perpetuity, the entire length of the canal, together with the tramroad, to their arch rivals, the railway companies and the Leeds & Liverpool Canal Company. The North End of the canal went to the Lancashire & North Western Railway Company, and the South End went to the Leeds & Liverpool Canal Company. As for the tramroad itself, which had already been leased some 27 years earlier, the Act allowed the closure

# The Declining Years of the Tramroad

View from the Old Vicarage looking over Avenham Park – 1863.
In the distance can be seen the Tramroad Bridge and Engine House. The white building is Jackson's Farm. (*Harris Museum*)

of the length between Bamber Bridge and Preston thus negating the problems with maintaining the tramroad bridge.

The railway company commenced removing the cast iron plates, stockpiling them at various locations before putting them to use elsewhere or alternatively selling them off for scrap. At Walton Summit a substantial quantity of plates had been rusting away for several years, and proved too much of a temptation for one Thomas Entwistle, who helped himself to them on three occasions during November 1872. He received £3 per ton for his booty from Frank Foster whose foundry was situated in Hope Street,

---

### PROBABLE DEMOLITION OF THE TRAMWAY

The solicitors to the London and North-Western Railway Company and the Lancaster Canal Company has given notice to the owners of the property abutting the tramway that powers will be sought by a bill, entitled the "Lancaster Canal Transfer Bill" intended to be brought into Parliament next session, to relinquish so much of the tramway as extends from the north side of Fishergate, in Preston, to the south side of the turnpike road at Bamber-bridge, and the works connected therewith with a view to disposing of the site. We understand that the Corporation of Preston, will endeavour, in case the bill should pass, to obtain that portion of the site which runs behind Ribblesdale-place to the tramway bridge across the Ribble, for the purpose of improving and extending the promenades at Avenham.

*Lancaster Gazette 19th December 1863*

## The Old Tram Road

Preston. Unfortunately for Entwistle, word got around of his activities and he was apprehended by the Police in North Road and subsequently sent down.

With around 40,000 cast iron plates to dispose of, no doubt the railway company were obliged to prosecute a number of like-minded entrepreneurs before they could be used or sold off lawfully.

In July 1872, a deal was struck between the railway company and Preston Corporation. The corporation offered Syke Road, which ran from the bottom of Garden Street and via a tunnel under the southern end of the station to Waltons Parade, in exchange for the length of tramroad between Preston and Carr Wood.

The Preston Guardian published on 31 May 1873 offered a prophetic view of the future use of the tramroad bridge:

> possibly at some remote period of the world's history, or the town's, it may give place to a handsome structure doing alike credit to the Corporation and the locality. It will form – in fact, it now forms, the approach to what will, before many years elapse, prove one of the finest promenades in the whole country-side. The walk up the tram-road, in the direction of Bamber Bridge, has been planted for 1,300 yards – the extent of the Corporation property – with young limes, which have already taken kindly to the soil, and given promise of vigorous life. A leafy avenue of two-thirds of a mile in length will in the course of years be here found. With regard to Carr Wood, which bounds the eastern-side of the walk, it has been contemplated to form it into a skating pond for the south and west of the town.

Local traffic continued to use the remainder of the tramroad to carry coal from what was now the Leeds & Liverpool Canal to the factories and mills in Bamber Bridge. This shortened form of the tramroad operated successfully for a further seventeen years until the progress of the railways made its continued existence unprofitable, whereupon an Act was passed on 21 July 1879 allowing the tramroad to be finally closed.

The buildings were demolished and the plates were taken up and weighed in for scrap. The stone sleepers were of little value and were left insitu, with the local farmers and house holders helping themselves whenever a wall or road needed to be constructed.

The plates to the north of Fishergate were left undisturbed until 1884, when these too were removed when the Lancashire & Yorkshire Railway began enlarging and modifying the Fishergate tunnel to form a vehicular access from Corporation Street to its Butler Street Goods Yard.

The North End of the Lancaster Canal was sold outright to the London & North Western Railway which led to the Lancaster Canal Company being finally wound up on 1 January 1886.

After the outstanding dividends were paid out, there remained the sum of £101 4s 10d which was used to strike a set of commemorative medals.

## The Old Tram Road Today

Over one hundred and thirty years have passed since the last train of waggons was hauled between Preston and Walton Summit, and much of the original line has now disappeared beneath the conurbation of Central Lancashire New Town. Today only the section between the River Ribble and Todd Lane North is easily recognisable and open to the public. Indeed this length seems destined to remain in perpetuity having recently been surfaced and designated a cycle track.

All traces of the tramroad at its Preston terminus have been obliterated by a series of commercial and residential developments. Likewise the Bamber Bridge section now lies beneath numerous residential estates. The southern end has fared no better, with the warehouses and infrastructure of Walton Summit industrial estate wiping out all trace of what went before.

Although little remains today, it is still possible to trace the line of the tramroad with the aid of old Ordnance Survey maps and a good imagination. The most helpful feature in identifying the route is the quick thorn hedges which, although planted nearly two hundred years ago, are still growing robustly. Apart from the thorn hedges, there are a few physical remains which can still be seen.

The tunnel beneath Fishergate which now serves as an access to the Fishergate Centre car park is on the line of the original tramroad tunnel although its entrance, instead of running parallel to the relatively recently constructed Corporation Street, ran in a direct line to the canal basin which was situated to the rear of the newly erected 'Aldi' store and Railtrack's Ladywell House.

The Tramroad south of the Old Tram Bridge – 1993.
South Ribble Council carry out works to the old track bed to reinstate the walking surface. This length has now been surfaced with bitmac to form a route for both walkers and bike riders. (*A.Iley*)

## The Old Tram Road

The Old Tramroad looking west from Todd Lane North – 1998.
The southern limit of the tramroad now forming a pedestrian/cycle route into Preston. (S.B.)

The Old Tramroad Looking East from Todd Lane North – 1968.
The bed of the Tramroad ran along a low embankment at this point. The thorn hedges planted to delineate the Tramroad are still growing robustly almost 200 years later. (S.B.)

# The Old Tram Road Today

Stone Bridge Abutment at Garden Street – near the Fishergate Centre Car Park – 1998. One of the few remaining relics. The stonework supported a timber bridge which carried the Tramroad across Garden Street at this point. The waggons would have passed through the bedrooms of the terraced property opposite, which was erected following the demise of the Tramroad. (S.B.)

The most substantial monument to the tramroad is provided by a stone bridge abutment constructed to support the timber decking which carried the dual track across Garden Street. This is sited near the Garden Street entrance to the Fishergate Centre Car Park.

The Avenham Incline slope remains, although all traces of the engine house and its associated reservoirs have long since disappeared under the landscape.

According to the Preston Guardian published on 31 May 1873, the remains of the engine house were put to good use in forming the new Avenham Park: 'All the massive stone bed of the engine house has been worked into steps, of which in various directions there are some half dozen new flights.'

The Old Tram Bridge is now built of precast concrete sections to the same pattern of the original timber structure, demonstrating the soundness of the original design. If one looks carefully into the river bed at low tide, one or two stone sleepers can be seen. These are easily identified by the two holes bored into them in order to receive the oak pegs to which the plates were spiked.

The tree lined walk to the south of the river has recently been surfaced, and now forms a cycle-way. The embankment itself was constructed to carry the tramroad but the tall lime trees which flank its banks were planted by the Victorians. If one looks to the right, at the bottom of the embankment, the original quick thorn hedge can be seen. Its twin, planted to mark the eastern boundary, lies some distance away from the toe of the embankment. Presumably this eastern boundary allowed sufficient room for the future canal to be constructed upon.

A flight of steps sited near the Old Engine House in Avenham Park – 1998. The stone foundations of the Engine House were used to construct flights of steps, as the Corporation saught to transform the area from pastureland into a municipal park. (S.B.)

The Penwortham incline is situated at the south side of the valley near the end of Factory Lane. The present route is that of the diversion, established to eliminate the engine worked inclined plane, and is of a gradient suitable for horses to work. The original slope of the inclined plane can still be made out (easier to see in winter) if one looks to the left down into the residential park. The site of the old winding house is now occupied by recently erected chalets positioned adjacent to the route near the top of the hill. At this point the adjacent, abandoned railway is separated from the tramroad by a stone wall. At the time of writing, the wall is being repaired, and a number of stone sleepers were found to have been incorporated in the original structure. I understand that these will be reinstalled as part of the refurbishment process.

Stone Sleepers forming the wall between the Old Tram Road and the disused railway near Factory Lane – 1998. Photographed during recent refurbishment works. (S.B.)

# The Old Tram Road Today

At Bamber Bridge, the tramroad crosses Station Road near the McKenzie Public House. To the south of the Mckenzie stood the village blacksmith's, with the tramroad passing between the two buildings. The smithy was ideally sited to afford convenient maintenance facilities for the tramroad waggons and horses and is still standing today offering the same service to the motor car under the banner of 'Autosave'.

Formerly known as Tramway Garage, the business was extended in 1990 over the route of the tramroad. Careful excavation of the site revealed a complete set of stone sleepers, at a depth of 7ft 3ins below the modern ground level, forming the dual road. In some instances the cast iron plates were still in position, with cobblestones forming a walking surface brought up level with the top of the flange. A channel was formed in pebbles to either side of the road bed to carry the rainwater run-off from the tramroad to the drainage system. Between the plates, two oak barrels were found sunk into the ground. It is thought that these would have been filled with water to allow the horses to refresh themselves whist in harness.

During the dig, evidence was found of two spur roads, one leading into the smithy from the east and the other into a coal yard across the other side of Station Road, also from the east.

After all the details were recorded, the sleepers were lifted to enable the new building to be constructed. The stones now have a new resting place on Worden Park, Leyland near the miniature railway track.

South Ribble Museum has an example of the type of plate likely to have been installed at the turnpike crossing. The plate has a flange of a constant depth and has no rib cast on its underside and is generally of a more robust construction than those used elsewhere. This type of rail would have been ideally suited to withstand the constant battering meted out by the turnpike traffic as it trundled between Preston and Wigan.

Gough Lane in Walton Summit is on the line of the tramroad, and until recently boasted the only remaining building associated with it. The Duke of Devonshire's weigh-bridge stood half way down on the left hand side. Sadly the site is now occupied by a modern structure which appears to be constructed on the original stone foundations of the old weigh bridge house.

As for the Walton Summit incline, a tarmac footpath climbing from the south side of Clayton Brook Road marks its approximate line, with the area of public open space at its summit being the site of the tramroad's southern terminus.

No doubt there are several examples of the cast iron plates in private collections, with perhaps hundreds of examples of the stone sleepers having been put to good use in people's gardens. However, the public collection of artifacts, besides the sleepers on Worden Park, comprise of

Iron Gad Nail.
Close up of an iron gad nail set in a stone sleeper. (S.B. – 1998)

# The Old Tram Road

Bamber Bridge Smithy, Station Road.
Situated next-door to the McKenzie Public House. The building now houses Autosave.
(*B. Dutton*)

Stone sleepers adjacent to the McKenzie Public House – 1990.
This photograph taken during works to Autosave shows several stone sleepers lying in their original positions. (*B. Dutton*)

*The Old Tram Road Today*

Section of Tramroad recreated using stone sleepers recovered from Autosave. Now sited on Worden Park, Leyland, near the miniature railway. (S.B. – *1998*)

three cast iron plates in South Ribble Museum, with a further plate and cast iron wheel recovered from the Ribble together with a scale model of a tramroad waggon displayed in the Harris Museum; not much to mark the existence of the tramroad, but after all it was only intended to be a temporary expedient and it was a long time ago.

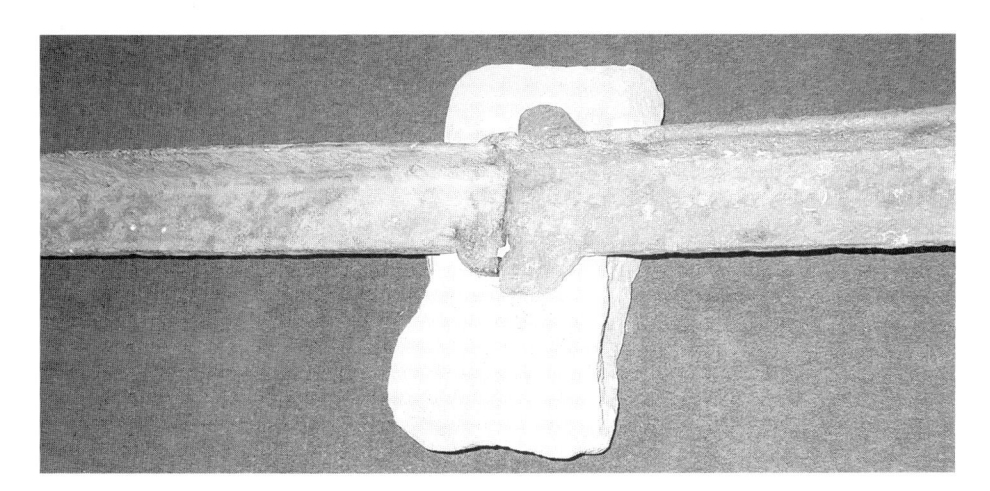

Type of plate likely to have been installed at the Turnpike Crossing (Station Road). The plates which crossed the turnpike would have suffered a tremendous buffeting by the nineteenth century traffic plying between Preston and Wigan, and it was normal practice to install a more robust type of plate at these points. Compared here with a standard plate, the crossing plate is on the left. The rails and sleeper depicted are stored at South Ribble Museum. (S.B. – *1998*)

## John Rennie (1761-1821)

In 1791, when John Rennie was approached by the Lancaster Canal Company, he was at the beginning of an illustrious civil engineering career which would see him constructing some of the worlds greatest and most enduring structures. The previous year he had been contracted to survey a line for the Kennet and Avon, and earlier the same year a line for the Rochdale Canal Comany, although this was subsequently installed by Jessop. However, the Lancaster Canal was the first of Rennie's canal projects to commence construction on site.

He was born on 7 June 1761 at Phantassie, Haddingtonshire in Scotland the youngest son of a farmer, James Rennie.

The Phantassie estate supported a number of small factories, one of which was owned by a man called Andrew Meikle who was a millwright by trade but who also spent much of the time inventing and building mechanical devices, his most famous invention being the threshing machine which he patented in 1788.

Young John spent much of his childhood around Meikle's factory where he learnt the rudiments of being a millwright and fuelled his growing interest in all things mechanical. This led to him setting up his own business in 1779.

Whilst confident in his own ability to design and construct mechanical devices, Rennie realised that he needed some formal academic training, and in 1780 he gained a place at Edinburgh University where he remained until 1783.

By 1784, he was looking to broaden his experience and to this end set out on horseback to tour the country's greatest engineering works. At Birmingham he called on James Watt in search of employment. The firm of Boulton and Watt manufactured steam engines and much of their work was associated with the mechanisation of various types of mills. John Rennie was hired on account of his millwright training and his exceptional talent for innovative engineering which would enable him to harness the power of Watts engines to the complex mechanics of the mills.

As a result of a verbal agreement with Watt, Rennie never built his own steam engines and as time passed, the emphasis of his work began to shift from that of mechanical to one of civil engineering.

In 1790, he embraced the world of canal engineering and quickly established himself as a leader in that field. Although he had a great belief in his own ability, he distrusted the ability of others and as a result carried out most of the surveys, design work and preparation of estimates himself. When it came to the realisation of his designs on site, he insisted that the various companies employed only the best people in the key positions, and that those persons be rewarded handsomely for their labours. By this method, Rennie could ensure that his designs would be constructed in the best possible manner.

He went on to build numerous canals, bridges, aqueducts and harbours in this country and abroad, working alongside many of the great engineers of the period including the likes of Telford, Jessop and Robert Stevenson.

As for John Rennie's physical appearance, his son described him as:

> very dignified and imposing. He was nearly 6ft 4ins tall, extremely well proportioned and powerfully built, and in his prime could and did walk 50 miles in a day without fatigue and could easily lift 3cwts. upon his middle finger. His head was extremely fine and majestic with a broad oval open countenance, large expressive blue eyes, high developed forehead. prominent nose slightly curved, with proportionate mouth and chin, and splendid luxurious auburn hair.

The structures erected by John Rennie during his lifetime were well designed and solidly built and have stood the test of time well. He was a precise and conscientious engineer regularly visiting the scene of his works to familiarise himself with any localised problems which may affect his designs.

He was dedicated to his chosen profession, and worked long hours and travelled great distances in the course of his working life. Although he was a strong man capable of great endurance, it is likely that the punishing schedule he set himself and the every day stress associated with constructing some of the worlds greatest structures conspired to shorten his life. He died at his home in Stanford Street, London after a short illness, on the afternoon of 4 October 1821 and was buried at St Paul's Cathedral.

The lasting monument to his endeavours on the Lancaster Canal is the elegant stone aqueduct bridging the River Lune at Lancaster which is still regarded as one of the finest structures of its kind in the country. An inscription, in Latin, appears on the south west side of the aqueduct which when translated reads: 'Things, that were wanting, are brought together, things remote are connected; rivers themself meet by the assistance of art, to afford new objects of commerce.'

## William Jessop (1745-1814)

William Jessop was retained by the company to survey the Preston end of the proposed tramroad. This was a good move by the committee for he was an engineer with a vast knowledge of every aspect of canal engineering and a keen interest in the use of the new 'wonder' material cast iron.

He had been taught his profession by one of the most influential engineers of the early canal age, John Smeaton, who is best known today for his efforts in constructing the Eddystone Lighthouse.

William Jessop's father Josias, a shipwright by trade, was employed to maintain the timbers of the wooden lighthouse up to its destruction by fire on the night of 1 December 1755. John Smeaton was engaged to design and supervise the replacement stone lighthouse and Josias Jessop was kept on to act as resident engineer for the works through to its successful completion in 1759. By the end of the contract, Smeaton and Jessop had become good friends. So much so that, when Josias died shortly

## The Old Tram Road

afterwards at an early age, Smeaton took it upon himself to become his son's guardian and set about teaching him the principles of civil engineering.

In 1767, when aged 23, William Jessop was engaged as surveyor engineer for a scheme to make navigable the River Ure from its confluence with the River Ouse, above York, to Ripon, the top two miles involving the cutting of a parallel canal. This was the start of a long and illustrious career which saw Jessop employed in various capacities on many of the major civil engineering projects throughout Britain, rising ultimately to become the most eminent engineer of his time.

Jessop and Smeaton maintained a close liaison, until Smeaton's death in 1792, and worked together on a number of undertakings including the surveying of a line for the Aire and Calder Navigation in 1772.

In 1791, Jessop became a partner in the Butterley Ironworks near Derby and, in common with many engineers of that period, sought to introduce cast iron as an alternative to stone and timber in the civil engineering field.

Towards the end of the eighteenth century, Jessop was engaged as engineer for the Ellesmere Canal and appointed under him as assistant engineer was a young former stonemason called Thomas Telford. The canal had to cross the River Dee, and it was originally intended to achieve the crossing via a low masonry aqueduct which would require lockage at either side of the valley. However, as a result of Jessop's recommendations, the aqueduct was eventually constructed of cast iron at a high level thus eliminating the need for lockage.

Jessop's aqueduct was not the first to be constructed of cast iron but he no doubt influenced his former assistant Thomas Telford in his decision to use cast iron to span the River Tern after the original masonry structure had been swept away, thus creating the first ever cast iron aqueduct.

A significant event occurred in 1801, when a canal was proposed for the Wandle Valley connecting Croydon to Wandsworth on the Thames. Jessop was consulted, whereupon he pointed out to the promoters that a canal would be impracticable, for the quantity of water required to be syphoned off the River Wandle to serve the canal would leave the numerous mills throughout the area without power. As an alternative, he suggested that a tramroad should be constructed or as he called it an 'iron railway'. The committee accepted Jessop's recommendations and an act was subsequently applied for and passed, not for a canal but for the 'Surrey Iron Railway', which led to the formation of the first public railway.

William Jessop today is looked on as the link between the 'amateur' engineer of the early eighteenth century and the professional engineer of the nineteenth century. He developed the ideas and expertise of John Smeaton, and passed his knowledge on to the next generation in the form of John Rennie and Thomas Telford, both of whom he worked with and advised on many occasions. He died in 1814 long before the decline of the canals and the coming of the steam locomotive but there is no doubt that his work in promoting the use of tramroads was instrumental in the development of the railways after his death by the engineers who succeeded him.

# *A Chronology of Events*

Key: Events affecting the Lancaster Canal in bold type
Selected local events in normal type
*Selected national events in italic type*

1757  *Sankey Navigation completed.*
1761  *Duke of Bridgewater's canal halves cost of coal to Manchester*
1764  *James Hargreaves invents the 'Spinning Jenny'.*
1769  *Richard Arkwright patents the 'Spinning Frame'.*
1770  **Act of Parliament granted for the Leeds & Liverpool Canal.**
1771  Stagecoach commenced running between Preston, Wigan and Warrington
      First Preston cotton mill built in Moor Lane.
1771  **Meeting of businessmen at Lancaster Town Hall resolve to initiate survey of canal route.**
1772  **Robert Whitworth submits survey of canal route to the committee which is subsequently rejected.**
      **Liverpool end of Leeds & Liverpool Canal reaches Parbold and changes its route to link with the River Douglas.**
1775  *James Watt perfects the steam engine.*
      *First steam ship built.*
1779  *First iron bridge constructed at Coalbrookdale.*
      *Samuel Crompton Invents the 'Spinning Mule'.*
1779  Walton road bridge built (completed 1781)
1780  Preston Town Hall fell.
1780  **Leeds & Liverpool Canal is extended to Wigan.**
1781  *George Stephenson is born.*
1782  New Town Hall opened.
1789  New House of Correction, Church St opened.
1791  John Horrocks' 'Yellow Factory' opened.
1791  **Lancaster Canal Committee meet again to initiate a further survey.**
1792  *Sir Richard Arkwright dies.*
1792  **John Rennie submits his survey which is subsequently accepted, and an Act of Parliament is obtained for the Line. Contractors appointed to construct the canal between Tewitfield and Ellel.**
1793  **Contractors appointed to construct the canal between Ellel and Ray Lane (Catterall) and also between Barkhill and Nightingales.**
1794  **John Rennie prepares plan for a stone aqueduct over the River Lune which is accepted. Work starts on the foundations in January. William Cartwright appointed as assistant resident engineer to supervise.**
1795  **Lune Aqueduct foundation piers completed in July.**
1796  **Part of the completed South End takes a little coal traffic.**
      Leeds end of the Leeds & Liverpool Canal reaches Burnley.
1797  **First section of the North End is opened on 22 November between Tewitfield and Spitall Moss.**
1798  **South End of Lancaster Canal opened from Bark Hill (above Wigan) to Knowsley Wharf (Chorley).**
      **Packet boats begin running between Preston and Lancaster.**
1799  **William Cartwright is appointed Resident Engineer for the remainder of the canal.**
      **South End of canal opened up to Clayton Green except for the Whittle Hills tunnel.**

*The Old Tram Road*

|      | Cartwright's opinion sought on uniting the North and South Ends of canal by tramroad. James Monk of Leeds & Liverpool committee submits proposal to link North End of canal to Leeds & Liverpool Canal via River Douglas Navigation, this is rejected. |
|------|---|
| 1800 | Act of Parliament obtained to raise more money to finance further canal work including the construction of a tramroad. |
| 1801 | *Richard Trevithick builds a steam road carriage.* |
| 1801 | During May, Rennie and Jessop, Cartwright, Gibson submit separate proposals for an Aqueduct crossing the Ribble. The committee reject plans in favour of tramroad. |
| 1802 | Tramroad bridge completed. |
|      | Extension of canal from Spitalls Moss to Preston Basin completed. |
| 1803 | Whittle Hills tunnel completed. |
|      | Tramroad completed uniting the North and South Ends of the canal. |
| 1804 | William Cartwright dies 19 January. |
| 1804 | John Horrocks dies. |
| 1805 | *Battle of Trafalgar.* |
| 1806 | *I.K.Brunel is born.* |
| 1810 | Seven locks constructed at Johnson's Hillock. |
|      | Agreement with Leeds & Liverpool to use the Lancaster Canal between Johnson's Hillock and Bark Hill. |
| 1811 | *Luddites destroy machinery in Nottinghamshire and Yorkshire.* |
| 1813 | *William Hedley builds a locomotive 'Puffing Billy'.* |
| 1814 | *The Times is printed by steam.* |
| 1815 | *Battle of Waterloo.* |
| 1816 | Preston first lighted with gas. |
|      | Last person to be pilloried at Preston Market Place. |
| 1817 | Hincaster tunnel completed on Christmas day. |
| 1819 | Eight locks finished construction at Tewitfield. |
|      | Canal completed between Tewitfield and Kendal. |
|      | Act of Parliament obtained to raise money for the Glasson Dock branch. |
| 1819 | *Peterloo Massacre.* |
|      | *Queen Victoria is born.* |
| 1822 | More powerful steam engine installed to the Avenham Incline on the tramroad. |
| 1823 | 72 Coaches run in and out of Preston in one day. |
| 1824 | Preston Corn Exchange opens. |
| 1825 | *Stockton & Darlington Railway opens* |
| 1826 | Serious riots, power looms destroyed. |
| 1826 | Glasson Dock branch of Lancaster Canal Completed. |
| 1827 | Whittle Hills tunnel collapses twice. |
|      | Twyford and Wilson propose link between North End of canal to the Douglas Navigation via booms across the Ribble, cutting out the tramroad. The proposal is rejected. |
| 1829 | First steamer on the Ribble. |
| 1829 | *Rainhill Trials take place to establish the locomotive to work the Manchester & Liverpool Railway.* |
| 1830 | Preston Cock Pit closed for fighting. |
|      | 81 Coaches in and out of Preston in one day. |
| 1831 | Act of Parliament obtained for Preston & Wigan Railway. (Directors appointed at a meeting in the Red Lion Inn, Church Street). Canal committee approach George Stephenson to look into ways of making the tramroad more efficient. |
| 1833 | Swift packet boats commence running between Lancaster and Kendal in anticipation of competition from the railways. |
|      | The Water Witch started running daily on 2 July, leaving Kendal at 6:00 a.m. and arriving in Preston at 1:00 p.m. The return journey starting at 1:30 p.m. and arriving in Kendal at 8:45 p.m. |
| 1833 | Last horse race on Fulwood Moor. |

# A Chronology of Events

| | |
|---|---|
| 1834 | Launch of the *Enterprise*, the first steamboat to be built in Preston. |
| 1836 | Spinners strike. |
| 1836 | **Whittle Hills tunnel collapses again.** |
| 1837 | *Queen Victoria comes to the throne.* |
| 1837 | Bolton and Preston Railway leases tramroad. |
| | Bolton and Preston Railway obtain agreement to enter Preston via North Union line. |
| 1838 | North Union Railway opened Whittle Hills tunnel opened out in the middle. |
| 1840 | Lancaster & Preston Railway opens. |
| 1850 | Traffic agreement is reached – Lancaster Canal to carry coal, and Lancaster & Carlisle Railway to carry passengers. |
| 1850 | First stone laid to St Walburg's Church. |
| 1850 | *Telephone invented.* |
| 1851 | *First double decker bus is built and operated* |
| 1854 | Explosion on steam boat 'Victoria' in the Ribble, five dead, several injured. |
| 1854 | **Trials of 'The Dandy', the first and only screw steamboat on the Lancaster Canal.** |
| 1855 | Collision on the Ribble between the 'Lively' and the 'Jenny Lind'. four dead. |
| 1856 | **Extensive repairs to the tramroad bridge are required.** |
| 1858 | **Avenham incline winding house boiler renewed.** |
| 1859 | Bus service commences between Preston and Fulwood. |
| 1860 | The Old Factory at Moor Lane is demolished. |
| 1862 | Foundation stone is laid for the new town hall. |
| 1862 | **Tramroad bridge ceases to be used by canal traffic but the tramroad continues to be used for transporting coal from the South End of the canal to Bamber Bridge.** |
| 1863 | 4 and 5 November great floods occur in Preston. |
| 1864 | Leeds & Liverpool Canal lease South End of Lancaster Canal. |
| | London & North Western Railway lease North End of Lancaster Canal. |
| 1866 | 15 and 20 November great floods in the Preston area. |
| 1867 | 10 August fearful accident on the Longridge Railway, 70 persons injured. |
| | 3 October new Town Hall opened. |
| | Miller Park and Avenham Park opened. |
| 1868 | **Avenham incline engine house demolished.** |
| 1868 | First Hansom cab appears in Preston. |
| 1869 | 14 March, earthquake felt in Preston area. |
| 1870 | 6 August, roof of covered market collapses whilst under construction. |
| 1871 | 17 March, earthquake felt in Preston Area. |
| 1873 | **Belvedere is moved to the site of the Avenham incline engine house, to make room for the Earl of Derby's statue.** |
| 1874 | 20 February, railway collision at Euxton Junction; the limited mail train dashed into a standing coal train. The driver and stoker of the mail train were both killed and many passengers were injured. |
| | 3 November, the last public pump was removed from Fishergate. |
| 1875 | Covered market completed. |
| 1879 | **Act of Parliament obtained to close the remainder of the tramroad.** |
| 1879 | 20 March, the first electric tramway line is opened between Preston and Fulwood. |
| 1880 | 11 June, first telephonic line installed at Preston. |
| | 18 July, Preston New Central Station is opened. |
| 1885 | **London & North Western Railway Company purchase the Lancaster Canal** |
| 1886 | **Lancaster Canal Company is dissolved.** |
| 1968 | **Walton Summit Basin is filled in.** |
| 1993 | Work commences on converting parts of the old tramroad to a footway and cycle path. |
| 1997 | Proposal to connect North End of the Lancaster Canal to the rest of the network by a new canal (the first this century), the Ribble estuary and the River Douglas, given National Lottery Funding. |

# Bibliography

## Books & Periodicals

*Lancashires Early Industrial Heritage* – L.C.C
*Outlines of an Economic History of Lancaster 1800 to 1860* – M. M. Schofield (1951)
*Pennine Waterway* – Gordon Biddle (1977)
*A History of the Ribble Navigation From Preston to the Sea* – James Barron (1938)
*The Canals of North West England* Vol. 1 & 2 – C. Hadfield & G. Biddle (1973)
*Building The Lancaster Canal* – Robert Philpott (1983)
*The History of the Borough of Preston and its Environs* – C. Hardwick (1857)
*History, Directory & Gazetteer of Lancashire* Vol. 2 – Baines (1825)
*History of the English Railway* Vol. 1 – Francis (1851)
*A Compendious History & Description of the North Union Railway* – E. C. Buller
*Some Historical Notes on the Wigan Coalfield* – H. E. Clegg (1957)
*History of Preston A.D. 705 to 1883* – Hewitson
*Railways Around Preston* – Gordon Biddle (1992)
*The History of Preston in Lancashire* (1922)
*Watery Preston a Local Miscellany* – Paul Gadkin
*A Historical and Descriptive Account of the Town of Lancaster* (1811)
*A Five Month Tour Through the North of England* – Arthur Young (1770)
*The Rainhill Story. The Great Locomotive Trial* – Anthony Burton (1979)
*The Peak Forrest Tramway (1794–1936)* – D. Ripley
*The Canal Buiders* – Anthony Burton (1972)
*William Jessop, Engineer* – Charles Hadfield and A. W. Skempton
*Lancaster Gazette*
*Preston Pilot*
*Preston Chronical*
*Preston Guardian*
*Lives of the Engineers Vol 2 Smeeton and Rennie* – Samuel Smiles (1874)

## Plans and Documents Held in the Lancashire Record Office, Bow Lane, Preston

Design for a Weigh Machine for the Duke of Devonshire's Wharf on the Lancaster Canal
DDHE 69/3 – Plan and Explanatory Report of a Proposal to Connect the Leeds Liverpool Canal to the Lancaster Canal by the Douglas, Across the Ribble via. a Boom then Through to the Wyre with a Connection to the Lancaster Canal near Salwick (26th October 1827) by Twyford and Wilson
*The Lancaster Canal Tramroad* (1963) Journal of the Railway and Canal Historical Society – Gordon Biddle
Transcripts of Reports on the Lancaster Canal 1790–1800 – R. W. G. Bryant
DDX 1042/1 – Statement on Behalf of the Company of Proprietors of the Lancaster Canal Navigation in Opposition to the Lancaster and Preston Railway Bill (1837)

DDPC 2066 – *Robert Whitworth's Notebook* (1772–1774) showing estimates for the provision of a canal

DDX 973/1 – 132 Coloured Photographic Slides of the Tramroad and the Lancaster Canal Through to Johnsons Hillock. Taken Between 1967 and 1971

DDX 272/1-3 – Drawing of Aqueduct over the Ribble by William Cartwright (1801)

DDX 272/4 – Drawing of Aqueduct over the Ribble by William Jessop (1801)

DDPD 25/34 – Plan of Proposed Lancaster Canal by John Rennie (1792)

DDPA 3 – Report on the Proposed Lancaster Canal to the Committee (1792)

DDX 272/1-21– Photographs of Buildings, Bridges etc. on the Lancaster Canal 1792–1840

*Plans and Documents Held in the Harris Reference Library, Preston*

PQ 385 – Bolton Le Moors to Preston Railway Act (1837)

An Act for Authorising the Corporation of the Borough of Preston to Establish and Regulate Markets and Fairs, to Erect a Town Hall, an Exchange and Public Offices, and Make New Streets in Preston and for Other Purposes (1861)

An Act for Making and Maintaining a Navigable Canal from Kirby Kendal, in the County of Westmorland, to West Houghton, in the County Palatine of Lancaster (1790)

*Plans and Documents Held in the Lancaster Reference Library*

A Cursory View of a Proposed Canal from Kendal to Manchester

Cumberland & Westmorland Antiquarian & Archeological Society Vol xvlll n.s. 1917 pages 26–47 – John F. Curwen

*Plans and Documents Held at the Lancashire County Library H.Q., Preston*

N 26 – 385.5L The History of the Walton Summit Plate-way – Clement Edwin Stretton (1893)

N 26 – 914.272 GIB Walton Summit and Branch Canal the Last Phase – Winifred M. Gibbs (1970)

N 26 – LAN MOS 159 Farewell to the Summit – Railway & Canal Historical Society (4/5/1968)

The Mystery of the Disappearing Tramway Waggon – Railway & Canal Historical Society Occasional Paper 42

*Plans and Documents Held in the Public Record Office, Kew, London*

RAIL844

/3 (c1800) River Ribble Coloured Design with Sections by Thomas Gibson

/4 (c1800) Water Colour Design by William Cartwright

/5 (1801) Water Colour of Long Section by William Cartwright

/6 (1801) Water Colour Design Signed by J. Rennie and W. Jessop

/7(1801) Water Colour Plans and Sections Signed by Rennie and Jessop

/9/17 (UND) Draw Bridge at Preston

/9/25 (UND) Wooden Bridge with Single Track Railroad Buildings

/11/1 (UND) Engine House Coloured View

/11/14 (1805) Ribble Tunnel Plan of Foundations of Engine House

/13/2 (UND) Plan of Coal Hurreys at Preston Basin

/13/4 (UND) Proposed Yard off Fishergate

/18/3 (1801) Fishergate Preston Design Initialled W.C.

# The Old Tram Road

/24/1 (1818) Canal Company's Engine House Plan of Inclined Plane at. Signed Thomas Addison Junior

/24/2 (UND) Penwortham, Section of Inclined Plane at. see also /25

/24/3 (c1801) Plan of Walton Summit Basin

/24/4 (c1801) Plan of Walton Summit Basin

/24/5 (c1801) Plan of Walton Summit Basin

/24/6 (UND) Section of the Inclined Plane at Walton Summit

/25 (c1802) Penwortham, Section of Inclined Plane

26/1 (UND) Plan of Inclined Plane to Bamber Bridge

/26/2 (UND)Section of Same with Section of Stone Block Setting Inset

/26/3 (UND) Section of Proposed Inclined Plane at North End of Summit Level

/30/4 (UND) Steam Engine 'Glasgow Steam Engine'

/33/1 (1822) Land at Avenham Adjoining Railroad Wanted by the Canal Co.

/33/2 (UND) Land at Avenham Adjoining Railroad Belonging to W. Cross

/33/3 (UND) Land at Avenham Adjoining Railroad Near Avenham House

/36 (1805) Preston (Spittles Moss to River Ribble) Plan of Railroad with Canal and Lands Adjoining by William Miller

/37 (1830) Preston, Section of Proposed C. I. Railroad from Walton Summit to Preston

/38 (c1799) Plan and Section of Proposed C. I. Railroad from Preston (Lancaster level) to Summit Level near Clayton Green

/39 (1799) Another Section of the Above Signed William Cartwright

/40/1 (1802) Stone Block Settings, Section Signed W. C.

/40/2-3 (UND) Two More Sections of Stone Block Settings see also Rail 844/26/22

/41/1-2 (1813) Summit Level in Walton Le Dale, Two Plans Showing Branch Railroads, Basin and Wharfs at. by Thomas Addison/1

/51 (1840) Lancaster Canal Company's Tramroad in Preston Plan of Lands Adjoining Including Mr. Birchells Garden and Theatre off Fishergate

/52/1 (1801) Fishergate Hill, Preston Design for Tunnel by W. Cartwright

/52/2 (1801) Fishergate Hill, Preston Design for Tunnel by W. Cartwright

/52/3 (1801) Fishergate Hill, Preston Design for Tunnel by W. Cartwright

/55/16 (1833) Summit Plan of Addition

/88/2 (1801) Preston Basin, Plan Showing Field Names by W. Cartwright

/88/13 (1806) Preston, Plan of the Lancaster Canal Wharfs

/88/19 (UND) Preston, Plan of the Lancaster Canal Co. Land Situated Between Maudlands Bridge and Fishergate

/215 (1799) Plan and Statement to Raise Money to Unite the Ends of the Canal

/243 (1800-4) Letter Book

/264 (1800-4) Letter Book

## Miscellaneous

The Baxter Collection (21 photographs taken 1936–1960) – The Railway & Canal Historical Society